BLAKE'S Writer's Guide

for primary students

Merryn Whitfield

PASCAL PRESS

Blake's Writer's Guide

Reprinted 2010 (twice), 2011

ISBN: 978 1 92136 752 6

Published by Pascal Press
PO Box 250
Glebe NSW 2037
www.pascalpress.com.au
contact@pascalpress.com.au

Author: Merryn Whitfield
Publisher: Lynn Dickinson
Edited by Shelley Barons & Kerry Davies
Design and illustration by Janice Bowles

Printed by Green Giant Press

CONTENTS

AUSTRALIAN CURRICULUM CORRELATIONS - YEAR 3

LANGUAGE	ELABORATIONS	ACELA	PAGE
Language for interaction Examine how evaluative language can be varied to be more or less forceful	★ exploring how modal verbs, for example 'must', 'might',' or 'could' indicate degrees of certainty, command or obligation ★ distinguishing how choice of adverbs, nouns and verbs present different evaluations of characters in texts	1477	99–113
Text structure and organisation Understand how different types of texts vary in use of language choices, depending on their function and purpose, for example tense, mood, and types of sentences	★ becoming familiar with typical structural stages and language features of various types of text, for example narratives, procedures, reports, reviews and expositions	1478	36, 37, 38, 59, 60, 61–113
Understand that paragraphs are a key organisational feature of written texts	★ noticing how longer texts are organised into paragraphs, each beginning with a topic sentence/paragraph opener which predicts how the paragraph will develop and is then elaborated in various ways	1479	35, 37, 38, 41
Know that word contractions are a feature of informal language and that apostrophes of contraction are used to signal missing letters	★ recognising both grammatically accurate and inaccurate usage of the apostrophe in everyday texts such as signs in the community and newspaper advertisements	1480	5, 43, 106, 107
Expressing and developing ideas Understand that verbs represent different processes (doing, thinking, saying, and relating) and that these processes are anchored in time through tense	★ exploring action and saying verbs in narrative texts to show how they give information about what characters do and say ★ identifying different types of verbs and the way they add meaning to a sentence ★ exploring the use of sensing verbs and how they allow readers to know what characters think and feel ★ exploring the use of relating verbs in constructing definitions and descriptions ★ learning how time is represented through the tense of a verb and other structural, language and visual features	1482	40, 55, 65, 78, 81, 84, 90, 96, 99, 108, 111
Learn extended and technical vocabulary and ways of expressing opinion including modal verbs and adverbs	★ exploring examples of language which demonstrate a range of feelings and positions, and building a vocabulary to express judgments about characters or events, acknowledging that language and judgments might differ depending on the cultural context	1484	26, 30, 31, 32, 34, 38, 99–113
LITERATURE		**ACELT**	
Responding to literature Draw connections between personal experiences and the worlds of texts, and share responses with others	★ discussing relevant prior knowledge and past experiences to make meaningful connections to the people, places, events, issues and ideas in the text	1596	4, 10, 11, 108–110
Develop criteria for establishing personal preferences for literature	★ selecting and discussing favourite texts and explaining their reasons for assigning greater or lesser merit to particular texts or text types	1598	108
LITERATURE		**ACELT**	
Examining literature Discuss how language is used to describe the settings in texts, and explore how the settings shape the events and influence the mood of the narrative	★ identifying and discussing the use of descriptive adjectives to establish setting and atmosphere and to draw readers into events that follow	1599	20, 24, 54, 61–66
	★ discussing the language used to describe the traits of characters in stories, their actions and motivations: 'Claire was so lonely; she desperately wanted a pet and she was afraid she would do anything, just anything, to have one to care for'		

Discuss the nature and effects of some language devices used to enhance meaning and shape the reader's reaction, including rhythm and onomatopoeia in poetry and prose	★ identifying the effect of imagery in texts, for example the use of imagery related to nature in haiku poems ★ exploring how rhythm, onomatopoeia and alliteration give momentum to poetry and prose read aloud, and enhance enjoyment	1600	54, 55, 67–71
Creating literature Create texts that adapt language features and patterns encountered in literary texts, for example characterisation, rhyme, rhythm, mood, music, sound effects and dialogue	★ creating multimodal texts that combine visual images, sound effects, music and voice overs to convey settings and events in a fantasy world	1791	50–51, 54–55, 61–77
LITERACY		**ACELY**	
Texts in context Identify the point of view in a text and suggest alternative points of view	★ discussing how a text presents the point of view of the main character, and speculating on what other characters might think or feel ★ recognising that there is more than one way of looking at the same event and that stories seen through the eyes of one character privileges some aspects of the story over others ★ speculating about what other characters might think or feel and retelling the story from other perspectives (for example 'Cinderella' from the view of the 'Ugly Sisters')	1675	26, 31, 32, 34, 38 99-113,
Interpreting, analysing, evaluating Identify the audience and purpose of imaginative, informative and persuasive texts	★ identifying the author's point of view on a topic and key words and images that seem intended to persuade listeners, viewers or readers to agree with the view presented	1678	31, 32, 36–38, 61–113
Creating texts Plan, draft and publish imaginative, informative and persuasive texts demonstrating increasing control over text structures and language features and selecting print, and multimodal elements appropriate to the audience and purpose	★ using vocabulary, including technical vocabulary, relevant to the text type and purpose, and appropriate sentence structures to express and combine ideas ★ using appropriate simple, compound and complex sentences to express and combine ideas ★ selecting appropriate text structure for a writing purpose and sequencing content for clarity and audience impact	1682	10–19, 24–26, 28–30, 33, 34, 46–48
Reread and edit texts for meaning, appropriate structure, grammatical choices and punctuation	★ using glossaries, print and digital dictionaries and spell check to edit spelling, realising that spell check accuracy depends on understanding the word function, for example there/their; rain/reign	1683	35–41, 42–45

AUSTRALIAN CURRICULUM CORRELATIONS - YEAR 4

LANGUAGE	ELABORATIONS	ACELA	PAGE
Language for interaction Understand that social interactions influence the way people engage with ideas and respond to others for example when exploring and clarifying the ideas of others, summarising students' own views and reporting them to a larger group	★ recognising that we can use language differently with our friends and families, but that Standard Australian English is typically used in written school texts and more formal contexts ★ recognising that language is adjusted in different contexts, for example in degree of formality when moving between group discussions and presenting a group report ★ understanding how age, status, expertise and familiarity influence the ways in which we interact with people and how these codes and conventions vary across cultures ★ recognising the importance of using inclusive language	1488	3, 5
Understand differences between the language of opinion and feeling and the language of factual reporting or recording	★ identifying ways thinking verbs are used to express opinion, for example 'I think', 'I believe', and ways summary verbs are used to report findings, for example 'we concluded'	1489	31, 32, 78–98, 99–113
Text structure and organisation Understand how texts vary in complexity and technicality depending on the approach to the topic, the purpose and the intended audience	★ becoming familiar with the typical stages and language features of such text types as: simple narrative, procedure, simple persuasion texts and information reports	1490	10, 59–113
Understand how texts are made cohesive through the use of linking devices including pronoun reference and text connectives	★knowing how authors construct texts that are cohesive and coherent through the use of: pronouns that link back to something previously mentioned; determiners (for example 'this', 'that', 'these', 'those', 'the', 'his', 'their'); text connectives that create links between sentences (for example 'however', 'therefore', 'nevertheless', 'in addition', 'by contrast', 'in summary') ★identifying how a topic is described throughout a text by tracking noun groups and pronouns ★describing how texts connectives link sections of a text providing sequences through time, for example 'firstly', 'then', 'next', and 'finally'	1491	28–30, 39, 40, 41, 61–113
Recognise how quotation marks are used in texts to signal dialogue, titles and reported speech	★exploring texts to identify the use of quotation marks ★experimenting with the use of quotation marks in students' own writing	1492	22, 27, 42, 55, 62–63, 65–66, 76–77
Expressing and developing ideas Understand that the meaning of sentences can be enriched through the use of noun and verb groups and prepositional phrases	★ creating richer, more specific descriptions through the use of noun groups (for example in narrative texts, 'Their very old Siamese cat'; in reports, 'Its extremely high mountain ranges'	1493	20–22, 39–40, 50–51
Investigate how quoted (direct) and reported (indirect) speech work in different types of text	★investigating examples of quoted (direct) speech ('He said, "I'll go to the park today"') and reported (indirect) speech ('He told me he was going to the park today') and comparing similarities and differences	1494	22, 27, 42, 55, 62–63, 65–66, 76–77
Understand how adverbials (adverbs and prepositional phrases) work in different ways to provide circumstantial details about an activity	★ investigating in texts how adverbial phrases and clauses can add significance to an action, for example 'more desperately', 'he rose quietly and gingerly moved'	1495	63, 66, 77, 86, 92, 95
Incorporate new vocabulary from a range of sources into students' own texts including vocabulary encountered in research	★ building etymological knowledge about word origins (for example 'thermometer') and building vocabulary from research about technical and subject specific topics	1498	10,11, 12, 39–41, 51, 56

LITERATURE		ACELT	PAGE
Literature and context Make connections between the ways different authors may represent similar storylines, ideas and relationships	★ commenting on how authors have established setting and period in different cultures and times and the relevance of characters, actions and beliefs to their own time ★ comparing different authors' treatment of similar themes and text patterns, for example comparing fables and allegories from different cultures and quest novels by different authors	1602	32

AUSTRALIAN CURRICULUM CORRELATIONS - YEAR 4

LITERATURE		ACELT	PAGE
Responding to literature Discuss literary experiences with others, sharing responses and expressing a point of view	★sharing and discussing students' own and others' understanding of the effects of particular literary techniques on their appreciation of texts ★ drawing comparisons between multiple texts and students' own experiences. Commenting orally, in written form and in digital reviews on aspects such as: 'Do I recognise this in my own world?'; 'How is this text similar to or different from other texts I've read?'; 'How common is it to human experience in the real world?'; 'What new ideas does it bring?'; 'How do they fit with what I believe?'	1603	4, 10, 11, 61–113
Use metalanguage to describe the effects of ideas, text structures and language features of literary texts	★ examining the author's description of a character's appearance, behaviour and speech and noting how the character's development is evident through his or her dialogue and changing relationships and the reactions of other characters to him or her ★ sharing views using appropriate metalanguage (for example 'The use of the adjectives in describing the character really helps to create images for the reader')	1604	20–22, 24, 61–77
Examining literature Discuss how authors and illustrators make stories exciting, moving and absorbing and hold readers' interest by using various techniques, for example character development and plot tension	★ examining the author's description of a character's appearance, behaviour and speech and noting how the character's development is evident through his or her dialogue and changing relationships and the reactions of other characters to him or her * identifying pivotal points in the plot where characters are faced with choices and commenting on how the author makes us care about their decisions and consequences	1605	20–22, 24, 27, 33, 52–53, 61–77
Understand, interpret and experiment with a range of devices and deliberate word play in poetry and other literary texts, for example nonsense words, spoonerisms, neologisms and puns	★ defining spoonerisms, neologisms and puns and exploring how they are used by authors to create a sense of freshness, originality and playfulness ★ discussing poetic language, including unusual adjectival use and how it engages us emotionally and brings to life the poet's subject matter (for example 'He grasps the crag with crooked hands'/wee timorous beastie)	1606	54, 67–71
Creating literature Create literary texts that explore students' own experiences and imagining	★ drawing upon literary texts students have encountered and experimenting with changing particular aspects, for example the time or place of the setting, adding characters or changing their personalities, or offering an alternative point of view on key ideas	1607	52, 53, 64–66
Create literary texts by developing storylines, characters and settings	★ collaboratively plan, compose, sequence and prepare a literary text along a familiar storyline, using film, sound and images to convey setting, characters and points of drama in the plot	1794	10, 13–19, 20–22, 24, 28, 33
LITERACY		**ACELY**	
Interpreting, analysing, evaluating Identify characteristic features used in imaginative, informative and persuasive texts to meet the purpose of the text	★ describing the language which authors use to create imaginary worlds; how textual features such as headings, subheadings, bold type and graphic organisers are used to order and present information, and how visual codes are used, for example those used in advertising to represent children and families so that viewers identify with them	1690	5, 6, 13–19, 58–59, 61–113

AUSTRALIAN CURRICULUM CORRELATIONS - YEAR 4

LITERACY		ACELY	PAGE
Use comprehension strategies to build literal and inferred meaning to expand content knowledge, integrating and linking ideas and analysing and evaluating texts	* bringing subject and technical vocabulary and concept knowledge to new reading tasks, selecting and using texts for their pertinence to the task and the accuracy of their information * making connections between information in print and images * building and using prior knowledge and vocabulary * finding specific literal information * asking and answering questions * creating mental images * finding the main idea of a text * inferring meaning from the ways communication occurs in digital environments including the interplay between words, images, and sounds * making connections between the text and students' own experience and other texts	1692	4, 6, 10–11, 31, 56–60
Creating texts Plan, draft and publish imaginative, informative and persuasive texts containing key information and supporting details for a widening range of audiences, demonstrating increasing control over text structures and language features	* using research from print and digital resources to gather ideas, integrating information from a range of sources; selecting text structure and planning how to group ideas into paragraphs to sequence content, and choosing vocabulary to suit topic and communication purpose * using appropriate simple, compound and complex sentences to express and combine ideas * using grammatical features effectively including different types of verbs, adverbials and noun groups for lengthier descriptions	1694	11–19, 39–41, 46– 47
Reread and edit for meaning by adding, deleting or moving words or word groups to improve content and structure	* revising written texts: editing for grammatical and spelling accuracy and clarity of the text, to improve the connection between ideas and the overall flow of the piece	1695	35–45, 50–51

AUSTRALIAN CURRICULUM CORRELATIONS - YEAR 5

LANGUAGE	ELABORATIONS	ACELA	PAGE
Language for interaction Understand how to move beyond making bare assertions and take account of differing perspectives and points of view	* recognising that a bare assertion (for example 'It's the best film this year') often needs to be tempered by: using the 'impersonal it' to distance oneself (for example 'It could be that it is the best film this year'); recruiting anonymous support (for example 'It is generally agreed that it is the best film this year.'); indicating a general source of the opinion (for example 'Most critics agree that it is the best film this year.'); specifying the source of the opinion (for example 'David and Margaret both agree that it is the best film this year') and reflecting on the effect of these different choices	1502	31, 32, 99–113
Text structure and organisation Understand how texts vary in purpose, structure and topic as well as the degree of formality	* becoming familiar with the typical stages and language features of such text types as: narrative, procedure, exposition, explanation, discussion and informative text and how they can be composed and presented in written, digital and multimedia forms	1504	58–113
Understand how possession is signalled through apostrophes and how to use apostrophes of possession for common and proper nouns	* examining how conventions of punctuation are used in written and digitally composed lists and learning that in Standard Australian English it is not necessary to add another 's' to the end of a plural noun to indicate possession ('James' house'/ 'my parents' car')	1506	43
Expressing and developing ideas Understand how noun and adjective groups can be expanded in a variety of ways to provide a fuller description of the person, thing or idea	* learning how to expand a description by combining a related set of nouns and adjectives – 'Two old brown cattle dogs sat on the ruined front veranda of the deserted house'	1508	39–40
Understand the use of vocabulary to express greater precision of meaning, and know that words can have different meanings in different contexts	* moving from general, 'all-purpose' words, for example 'cut' to more specific words, for example 'slice', 'dice', 'fillet', 'segment'	1512	39–40, 51

AUSTRALIAN CURRICULUM CORRELATIONS - YEAR 5

LITERATURE		ACELT	PAGE
Responding to literature Use metalanguage to describe the effects of ideas, text structures and language features on particular audiences	* orally, in writing or using digital media, giving a considered interpretation and opinion about a literary text, recognising that a student's view may not be shared by others and that others have equal claims to divergent views	1795	31, 32, 61–113
Examining literature Recognise that ideas in literary texts can be conveyed from different viewpoints, which can lead to different kinds of interpretations and responses	* identifying the narrative voice (the person or entity through whom the audience experiences the story) in a literary work, discussing the impact of first person narration on empathy and engagement * examining texts written from different narrative points of view and discussing what information the audience can access, how this impacts on the audience's sympathies, and why an author might choose a particular narrative point of view	1610	6–7, 32, 64–66
Understand, interpret and experiment with sound devices and imagery, including simile, metaphor and personification, in narratives, shape poetry, songs, anthems and odes	* discussing how figurative language including simile and metaphor can make use of a comparison between different things, for example 'My love is like a red, red rose'; 'Tyger!, Tyger! burning bright, In the forests of the night'; and how by appealing to the imagination, it provides new ways of looking at the world	1611	54, 56, 67–71
Creating literature Create literary texts using realistic and fantasy settings and characters that draw on the worlds represented in texts students have experienced	* using texts with computer-based graphics, animation and 2D qualities, consider how and why particular traits for a character have been chosen	1612	61–77, 46–47
Create literary texts that experiment with structures, ideas and stylistic features of selected authors	* drawing upon fiction elements in a range of model texts - for example main idea, characterisation, setting (time and place), narrative point of view; and devices, for example figurative language (simile, metaphor, personification), as well as non-verbal conventions in digital and screen texts - in order to experiment with new, creative ways of communicating ideas, experiences and stories in literary texts	1798	20–22, 54, 55, 56, 61–77
LITERACY		**ACELY**	
Texts in context Show how ideas and points of view in texts are conveyed through the use of vocabulary, including idiomatic expressions, objective and subjective language, and that these can change according to context	* identifying the narrative voice (the person or entity through whom the audience experiences the story) in a literary work, discussing the impact of first person narration on empathy and engagement	1698	7, 31, 32
Interpreting, analysing, evaluating Identify and explain characteristic text structures and language features used in imaginative, informative and persuasive texts to meet the purpose of the text	* explaining how the features of a text advocating community action, for example action on a local area preservation issue, are used to meet the purpose of the text.	1701	61–113
Creating texts Plan, draft and publish imaginative, informative and persuasive print and multimodal texts, choosing text structures, language features, images and sound appropriate to purpose and audience	* using vocabulary, including technical vocabulary, appropriate to the type of text and purpose. Using appropriate grammatical features, including more complex sentences and relevant verb tense, pronoun reference, adverbials and noun groups for lengthier descriptions * selecting an appropriate text structure for the writing purpose and sequencing content according to that text structure, introducing the topic, and grouping related information in well-sequenced paragraphs with a concluding statement * using research from print and digital resources to gather and organise information for writing * using paragraphs to present and sequence a text	1704	10–22, 23–26, 28–30, 33–34, 41, 46–49
Reread and edit student's own and others' work using agreed criteria for text structures and language features	* editing for flow and sense, organisation of ideas and choice of language, revising and trying new approaches if an element is not having the desired impact	1705	35–41

AUSTRALIAN CURRICULUM CORRELATIONS - YEAR 6

LANGUAGE	ELABORATIONS	ACELA	PAGE
Language for interaction Understand the uses of objective and subjective language and bias	* understanding when it is appropriate to share feelings and opinions (for example in a personal recount) and when it is appropriate to remain more objective (for example in a factual recount) * differentiating between reporting the facts (for example in a news story) and providing a commentary (for example in an editorial)	1517	5, 31, 32
Text structure and organisation Understand how authors often innovate on text structures and play with language features to achieve particular aesthetic, humorous and persuasive purposes and effects	*exploring a range of everyday, community, literary and informative texts discussing elements of text structure and language features and comparing the overall structure and effect of authors' choices in two or more texts * examining different works by an author who specialises in humour or pathos to identify strategies such as exaggeration and character embarrassment to amuse and to offer insights into characters' feelings, so building empathy with their points of view and concern for their welfare	1518	61–113
Understand that cohesive links can be made in texts by omitting or replacing words	* noting how writers often leave out words that have already been mentioned (for example 'Tina ate three apples and Simon ate two. [apples]') * noting how writers often substitute a general word for a more specific word already mentioned, thus creating a cohesive link between the words (for example 'Look at those apples. Can I have one?') * recognising how cohesion can be developed through repeating key words or by using synonyms or antonyms * observing how relationships between concepts can be represented visually through similarity, contrast, juxtaposition, repetition, class-subclass diagrams, part-whole diagrams, cause-and-effect figures, visual continuities and discontinuities	1520	28, 39–40
Understand the uses of commas to separate clauses	* identifying different uses of commas in texts	1521	43, 65, 76, 79, 85, 103
Expressing and developing ideas Understand how ideas can be expanded and sharpened through careful choice of verbs, elaborated tenses and a range of adverbials	* knowing that verbs often represent actions and that the choice of more expressive verbs makes an action more vivid (for example 'She ate her lunch' compared to 'She gobbled up her lunch') * knowing that adverbials can provide important details about an action (for example 'At nine o'clock the buzzer rang loudly throughout the school.') * knowing the difference between the simple present tense (for example 'Pandas eat bamboo.') and the simple past tense (for example 'She replied.') *knowing that the simple present tense is typically used to talk about actions that happen regularly in the present (for example 'He watches TV every night.') or that represent 'timeless' actions, as in information reports (for example 'Bears hibernate in winter.') * knowing that there are various ways in English to refer to future time (for example 'She will call you tomorrow'; 'I am going to the movies tomorrow'; 'Tomorrow I leave for Hobart')	1523	40, 55, 56
Identify and explain how analytical images like figures, tables, diagrams, maps and graphs contribute to our understanding of verbal information in factual and persuasive texts	* observing how sequential events can be represented visually by a series of images, including comic strips, timelines, photo stories, procedure diagrams and flowcharts, life-cycle diagrams, and the flow of images in picture books * observing how concepts, information and relationships can be represented visually through such images as tables, maps, graphs, diagrams, and icons	1524	13–19, 49, 82–83, 85–86, 106– 107, 109– 110

AUSTRALIAN CURRICULUM CORRELATIONS - YEAR 6

LANGUAGE	ELABORATIONS	ACELA	PAGE
Investigate how vocabulary choices, including evaluative language can express shades of meaning, feeling and opinion	* identifying (for example from reviews) the ways in which evaluative language is used to assess the qualities of the various aspects of the work in question	1525	108– 110
LITERATURE		**ACELT**	
Responding to literature Analyse and evaluate similarities and differences in texts on similar topics, themes or plots	* exploring texts on a similar topic by authors with very different styles, for example comparing fantasy quest novels or realistic novels on a specific theme, identifying differences in the use of narrator, narrative structure and voice and language style and register	1614	32, 61–113
Examining literature Identify, describe, and discuss similarities and differences between texts, including those by the same author or illustrator, and evaluate characteristics that define an author's individual style	* exploring two or more texts by the same author, drawing out the similarities, for example subject or theme, characterisation, text structure, plot development, tone, vocabulary, sense of voice, narrative point of view, favoured grammatical structures and visual techniques in sophisticated picture books	1616	4, 6, 50–51
Identify the relationship between words, sounds, imagery and language patterns in narratives and poetry such as ballads, limericks and free verse	* identifying how language choice and imagery build emotional connection and engagement with the story or theme * describing how a character's experience expressed through a verse novel impacts on students personally, how the author controls the revelation of the experiences and how the verse story builds meaning to its climax when we understand the whole	1617	50–51, 53–56, 61–71
Creating literature Create literary texts that adapt or combine aspects of texts students have experienced in innovative ways	* creating narratives in written, spoken or multimodal/ digital format for more than one specified audience, requiring adaptation of narrative elements and language features * planning and creating texts that entertain, inform, inspire and/or emotionally engage familiar and less-familiar audiences	1618	52–55, 61–77
LITERACY		**ACELY**	
Interpreting, analysing, evaluating Analyse how text structures and language features work together to meet the purpose of a text	* comparing the structures and features of different texts, including print and digital sources on similar topics, and evaluating which features best aid navigation and clear communication about the topic	1711	58–113
Analyse strategies authors use to influence readers	* identify how authors use language to position the reader and give reasons	1801	5, 7, 31, 32, 50–57
Creating texts Plan, draft and publish imaginative, informative and persuasive texts, choosing and experimenting with text structures, language features, images and digital resources appropriate to purpose and audience	* creating informative texts for two different audiences, such as a visiting academic and a Year 3 class, that explore an aspect of biodiversity * using rhetorical devices, images, surprise techniques and juxtaposition of people and ideas and modal verbs and modal auxiliaries to enhance the persuasive nature of a text, recognising and exploiting audience susceptibilities	1714	13–19, 25–27, 29–31, 34, 46–49, 52–55

HOW TO USE THIS BOOK

Blake's Writer's Guide will provide you with the tools you need to be a successful writer. It will help you gain knowledge about the use of the different text types for different purposes and develop concepts about meeting the needs of your audience.

This guide contains:

- sections on each key element for developing good writing skills
- a comprehensive examination of the three broad groups of texts: imaginative, informative and argumentative
- annotated text examples accompanied by easy-to-follow lists of structure and language features
- a step-by-step guide through the writing process
- helpful hints for note-taking and researching topics
- guidelines for proofreading and editing your own texts
- a glossary with concise definitions for all the major terms (includes examples)
- tools every author needs to have and how to use them
- handy ideas for enhancing your texts with graphics and creative layouts

This guide is a vital reference for everyone who wishes to become a great writer.

ABOUT THE AUTHOR

Merryn Whitfield is an experienced educator currently working for the New South Wales Department of School Education in primary schools. Over the past two decades she has taught students from diverse cultural and socio-economic backgrounds across all stages K–6. Merryn has undertaken various educator positions including Assistant Principal; 'Minds in Motion' presenter; SCAN reviewer; and has led several teacher in-service courses in writing, grammar and NAPLAN analysis and testing.

Merryn has consistently worked with educators in public schools providing professional support and expertise, while guiding and encouraging changed classroom methodology and improved literacy practices. She is the author of many educational materials, including the best-selling *Excel – Parent's Guide to Primary English and Mathematics* and the award-winning *Targeting Writing Across the Curriculum series,* and has designed an extensive range of classroom resources for educators.

Her personal interests include her young family, water sports and reading widely.

INTRODUCTION

Do you know what writing is?

You might say that it is using a pen or pencil to make marks on paper, or perhaps you think of writing as typing on the computer. Writing for you may be using printing or cursive handwriting. All these are 'physical' expressions of writing, but the idea of writing, of using written language, is much more complicated.

Writing communicates with another person or group

The most important reason for anyone to write is to communicate with another person or group of people. However, unlike spoken language, writing is a process that happens over time and may have an unknown audience.

How are spoken language and written language different?

SPOKEN LANGUAGE	WRITTEN LANGUAGE
Usually has no permanent record.	Is permanent and can be kept over time.
Words and ideas can be corrected as the speaker communicates.	Words and ideas can't be easily changed once they have been published.
Used for immediate communication.	Used for communicating over time.
Is usually more informal – features poor grammar, incomplete sentences and can be interrupted.	Uses more complex language and grammatical patterns with punctuation.
A speaker can receive immediate feedback from his or her audience who also can participate actively in the communication.	A writer does not receive immediate feedback from his or her audience. The audience plays a more passive role in the communication.
A speaker does not use headings or graphic layouts.	A writer can use headings, illustrations and visual effects to aid communication.
Speech often uses slang and colloquial vocabulary.	Many forms of writing use formal language and complex vocabulary.

(Ager, S. 2008)

WHY WRITE?

Every time we write, we reveal something about ourselves: who we are, how we think, and how we interact with others, all because of the personal choices we make when we write.

As writers, we are constantly responding to the world around us. We are being social, communicating with others (audience) for a variety of different reasons (purpose). Whether it is a shopping list for the groceries, a sick note for school, or a letter of complaint, we have an expectation that our writing will be read and the person reading it will react in some way. The context of who we write for and what our purpose for writing is tells us how we will organise our writing: that is, what the tone will be (friendly or formal), what level of vocabulary will be used (slang or complex terminology), and what level of spelling and punctuation is appropriate (*C U L8R* or *I will see you later.*).

No matter what we write, in order to communicate meaningfully with others, our writing must make sense. To do this, we use grammar. [For more detailed information on grammar see *Blake's Grammar Guide* by Del Merrick.]

Often the process of writing starts with an idea or even a group of ideas. A writer has to take these scattered pieces and put them together in a logical and sequenced way. Writing is about making choices. What words should I use? How can I link these ideas or events? Does it make sense? Will the reader understand what I mean? These choices and self-reflective questions are a writer's constant companion. At every stage of the writing process writers are involved in rewriting and revising. We often write and rewrite our ideas in our minds, even before we put pen to paper. Writing involves a lot of trial and error as the writer searches for the right combination of words and ideas.

Perhaps most importantly, writing (both the process and the product) is something to be valued.

FORMAL AND INFORMAL WRITING

Formal writing is often used when the writer is unfamiliar with the audience, or when the writer wants their point to be taken thoughtfully. Formal writing is often used in official or professional situations. It can create a sense of confidence in the message. However, when formal language is used in an inappropriate situation, such as writing a note to a friend, it can make the writer seem stuck up or *arrogant*.

Formal writing is often used in official or professional situations.

Informal writing is the opposite. It is often used when the writer is familiar with the audience, or when the communication is relaxed and casual. Informal writing has a friendly feel to it and is more personal. It uses less complicated language and often includes slang. However, when informal language is used in an inappropriate situation, such as a letter to the Principal, it can make the writer seem *flippant* and not serious about the issue. (Martin, R. 2007, p.171)

Informal writing has a friendly feel to it and is more personal.

Formal letter

Mr Neville Candu
Hardly Primary School
Forgetaboutit

Dear Mr Candu,
I am very pleased to report to you that your school, Hardly Primary School, has been selected as one of the five finalists in the Regional Care For Your Playground Competition. You will receive notification of the inspection dates shortly. Thank you for entering. I wish your school the best of luck.

Kind regards,
Reginald Spring
Regional Competition Coordinator

Informal letter

Neville Candu
Hardly Primary School
Foregtaboutit

Hi Nev,
Well done mate! Your school has just made the finals of the Regional Care For Your Playground Competition. Isn't that great! Soon you'll get some more info about the inspections. I'm glad you gave it a go – good luck!

Bye,
Reggie

HOW CAN A WRITER HAVE A VOICE?

As a writer, you use your words to speak to your audience. They are your 'voice'. The words you choose, the details you include or leave out, how you start and finish your stories all add up to creating your special voice. The most important thing to remember is that your voice must be appropriate to the audience and purpose of your writing. Does your writing sound real, or does it sound fake? If you are writing a thank-you note to your aunty for your birthday present, do you sound cranky or pleased?

Just like a fingerprint, every writer has an individual voice, a tone or style that makes their writing 'sound' different to anyone else's.

How do you find your voice as a writer? That one is easy – write. The more your write, the more choices you make about your writing, the closer you get to defining what your voice is.

Some simple tips to help you along are:

- keep a diary
- watch the news and write about current affairs
- talk to others about important issues
- keep a word book to write down interesting words and phrases
- read well in order to write well.

Active voice

An active voice uses active verbs where the subject performs the action of the verb.

An active voice uses active verbs where the subject does the action.

Ben skipped across the playground.

Ben is the subject. He actively performs the verb (*skipped*); he is the one doing the skipping.

You will see active voice used most often in writing because it sounds stronger and more definite, where the character is in control.

Passive voice

A passive voice uses passive verbs where the subject receives the action of the verb; the subject does not do the action.

The motorbike was ridden dangerously around the sweeping bend.

The motorbike is the subject. The verb *was ridden* was not done by the motorbike but by someone or something else.

A passive voice uses passive verbs where the subject does not do the action.

Passive voice can be used in mystery or detective stories to conceal the agent of the action. It is also used in formal writing because it is impersonal. Using passive voice in a narrative can make a character seem weak and *indecisive*.
Be careful when using passive voice because it can sometimes confuse a reader if they do not know who or what is performing the action.

Who is speaking?

1 ***One of the many choices I have to make as a writer is how close I want to be to my audience and how close I want to be to the action and events in my writing.***

2 ***One of the many choices you as a writer have to make is how close you want to be to your audience and how close you want to be to the action and events in your writing.***

3 ***One of the many choices writers have to make is how close they want to be to their audience and how close they want to be to the action and events in their writing.***

Each of these three sentences says basically the same thing, but they are written using different pronouns.

Sentence 1 is written in **first person**, using personal pronouns such as *I* and *my*. It is obvious that it is the writer (me) speaking about myself. First person is quite useful when getting across a point of view or establishing opinions.

Sentence 2 is written in **second person**, using pronouns such as *you* and *your*. Second person establishes a personal link between the writer and the audience. Second person is quite useful in persuading others and advertising products.

Sentence 3 is written in **third person**, using pronouns such as *they* and *their*. It shows that the writer is writing about other things. Here the audience and the writer are remote from each other. Third person is quite useful when writing factual reports, explanations and descriptions.

The Writing Process

Step 1

Prewriting

- choose a topic
- set your audience
- understand your purpose
- gather information you need
- plan your ideas, layout and structure
- make notes and word banks

Step 2

Drafting

- write down your ideas
- use your prewriting notes to help
- write in sentences
- concentrate on the message
- mistakes can be fixed later

Step 3

Revising

- read and check your writing
- share your writing with others
- does it make sense?
- have you made good word choices?
- do you need to add more detail?
- do you need to make it more concise?
- have you met the needs of your audience?

This is a really important step.

Step 4

Editing/Proofreading

- fix any mistakes
- check your punctuation
- check your spelling
- get ready for your good copy

Step 5

Publishing

- write your final copy
- make it your best work
- make sure it is accurate
- make it look appealing
- include references/glossary /diagrams

Step 1 PREWRITING

As a writer, you will write best when you choose a topic that interests you.

Keep a notebook and jot down interesting words

Often when it comes time to write, you forget the good ideas you thought of yesterday or last week. So a simple tip is to keep a writing journal or notebook; somewhere to jot down interesting words, list creative topics, sketch outlines of characters, or list websites where you can access information.

Another important part of prewriting is to talk to others about your ideas. Your friends and classmates are writers themselves, as well as audiences, so share your ideas and you will usually get some constructive feedback that will help you organise your writing.

IDEA FRAME

Before you start writing, ask yourself these questions.

What is my topic?	Make it interesting. Make it informative.
What text type am I using?	Imaginative. Instructional. Argumentative.
What format will I use?	Brochure, website, picture book, poster, letter or something else?
Who is my audience?	Known or unknown? Teachers, parents, children?
Why am I writing?	To entertain. To inform. To instruct. To persuade. To explain.
Have I got the information and details I need?	Do I need to research using an encyclopaedia, atlas, books, internet?
How will it be published?	Read aloud, handwritten, computer generated, school website?
What do I need to include?	Diagrams, charts, illustrations, glossary, index, references.

RESEARCH YOUR TOPIC

Before you write, make a list of books and other resources you might find useful. As you read through the resources, jot down notes such as important facts and dates, interesting words, key steps in a process or sequence of events.

Your notes should be short and organised in a logical order so they make sense and you can understand them later when you are ready to write. Do not copy out large bits of writing. For a start, it takes a long time, and secondly, it is plagiarism. **Plagiarism** is stealing someone else's work and saying that it is your own.

Here are some key ideas for researching and note taking:

- understand exactly what information you need
- stay on the topic
- use a highlighter or underlining to identify information
- look at contents page and index to guide your search
- use headings and subheadings to guide your search
- find the main idea of each section or paragraph
- look for key topic words
- use abbreviations to keep notes short
- put the notes in order and use suitable headings
- use a graphic organiser to keep track of your research notes
- make a bibliography at the end.

REFERENCING

When you use notes from your research in your writing, you need to reference it, or make a note of it in your text. Sometimes this is done using footnotes[1]. Here you put a small number above the word and write more about it (to either provide further details, or to say where the information came from) at the bottom of the page. When using footnotes, make sure your numbers are in counting order throughout your writing. Footnotes are usually found in informative texts.

Sometimes you will reference your work by making a short note at the end of a sentence or paragraph. I have referenced my work in this way. You can see examples of it in the text samples for informative texts. Most authors do a lot of research before they write informative texts, so it is very important that we acknowledge where the information comes from, because nobody knows everything! You must reference information and ideas from books, brochures, newspapers and magazines, CD-ROM, websites, blog pages and movies, TV shows and the radio.

---

1 Footnotes: Rodney Martin, *Martin's Young Writers Guide*, 2007.

BIBLIOGRAPHY

Using a bibliography is another way of referencing your writing. It is a list of the resources that the writer has used to get any information for their own writing. It could be from another book, a magazine, a website, or a journal. A bibliography lists references in alphabetical order at the end of a book or piece of writing.

If you used information from this book, in your bibliography you would reference it like this:

Whitfield, Merryn, *Blake's Writer's Guide*, Pascal Press, Glebe, 2009

A complete bibliography can be found at the end of this book.

SKIM AND SCAN

Skimming and scanning is an important technique in note taking. You need to read a passage and highlight the important facts and details. You do not read every word, but look for key points such as dates and names. Look below at an example of this.

1 Highlight important areas of the text

The history of human involvement in Mars has been relatively short. Only recently has mankind taken up the challenge to explore the planet Mars and try to find out if it has ever, or could ever, support life.

Ever since recorded history began, mankind has been fascinated by what lay beyond Earth. Yet it wasn't until 1971 that an orbiting spacecraft called Mariner 9 observed Mars and found that there were a number of canyons and channels that appeared to have been carved out of the rocky landscape by floods and rivers.

Several years later, in 1976, two Viking spacecraft landed on Mars and took samples of soil. Unfortunately for scientists at the time, when they were analysed, the samples showed no evidence of life either then or in the past.

2 Take relevant notes

Notes on topic – Exploration of Mars

- human involvement has short history
- trying to find if Mars has/can supported life
- 1971 – spacecraft – Mariner 9 found canyons and channels carved by floods
- 1976 – Viking spacecraft took soil samples – no evidence of life

3 Rewrite notes in your own words in a draft paragraph

Human exploration of the Red Planet, Mars, has a brief history. The challenge is to find out whether Mars has ever, or could in the future, support life as we know it.
The Mars space program began in 1971 with the Mariner 9 spacecraft, which found canyons on the planet's surface that had been carved out by floods. Later, in 1976, the Viking spacecraft took samples of Martian soil, but found no evidence of life.

Remember, if you copy someone else's words – from a book, or the internet – it is plagiarism.

GRAPHIC ORGANISERS

Sometimes when taking notes, you do not have the text in front of you to highlight. So you need to write your notes on a separate piece of paper. There are many ways that writers can organise their notes. Different graphic organisers suit different text types. Here are a few examples.

Spider diagram *(useful for biographies, descriptions, reports, recounts)*

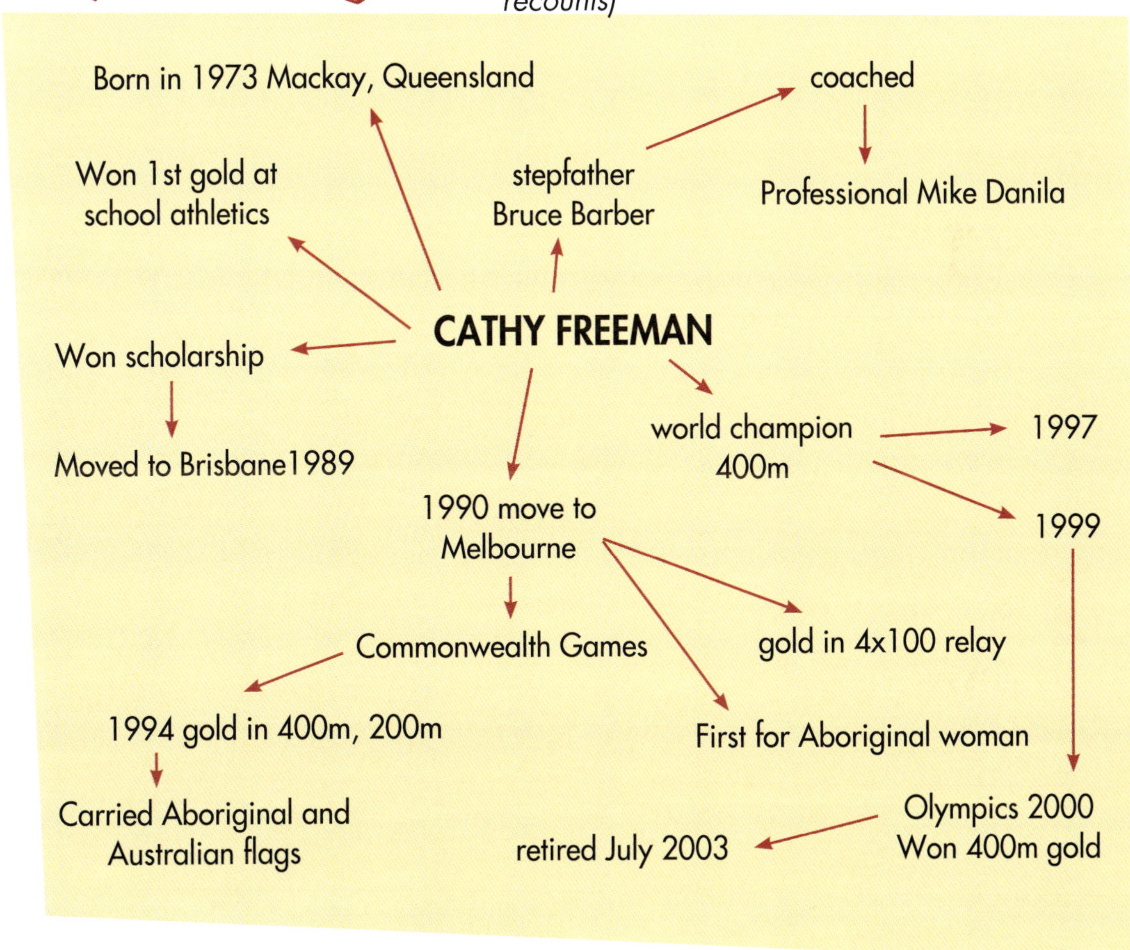

Flow chart *(useful for explanations)*

1. The queen bee lays one egg in each cell of the bee hive. They are cared for by nursery bees.
2. On the fourth day, the eggs hatch into larva. They look like small white sausages. They are fed nectar and pollen.
3. On the ninth day, each cell is covered with wax and the larva transforms into a pupa. The pupa does not eat.
4. On the 21st day, the adult worker bee emerges from the pupa and begins its life collecting pollen to make honey.

Timeline *(useful for recounts, narratives, procedures)*

1971 – Mariner 9	discovered canyons and channels
1976 – Viking spacecraft	took soil samples
1995 – Mars Pathfinder	sent out Sojourner to collect information
2001 – Odyssey Orbiter	sent by NASA
2004 – rovers Spirit and Opportunity	evidence of water once
2008 – Phoenix spacecraft	dug up soil – found frozen water

Concept map *(useful for reports, expositions, letters to the editor)*

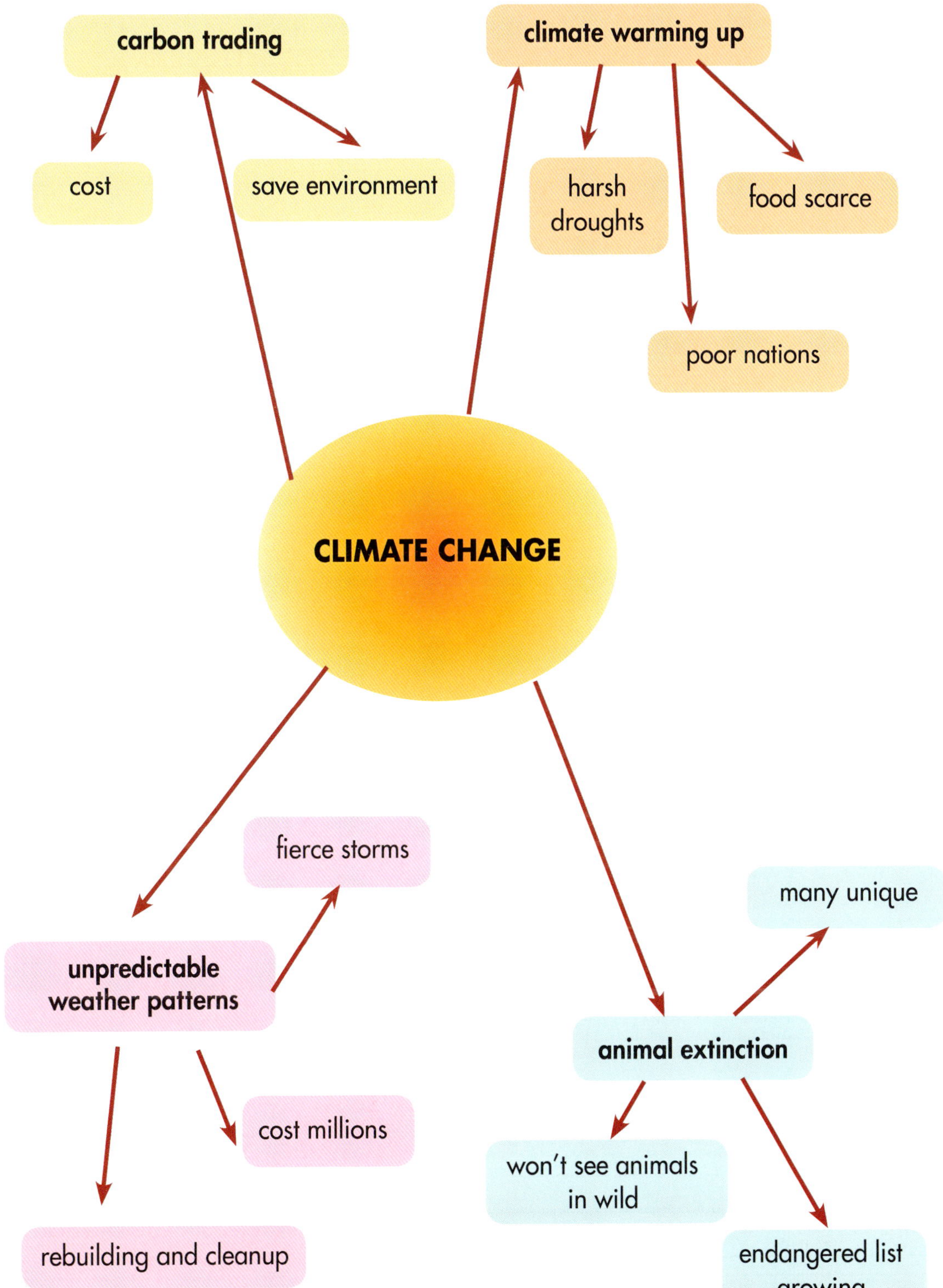

Brainstorm map *(useful for poetry, reports, descriptions)*

Story hill *(useful for narratives)*

Fishbone planner *(useful for explanations, expositions, discussions)*

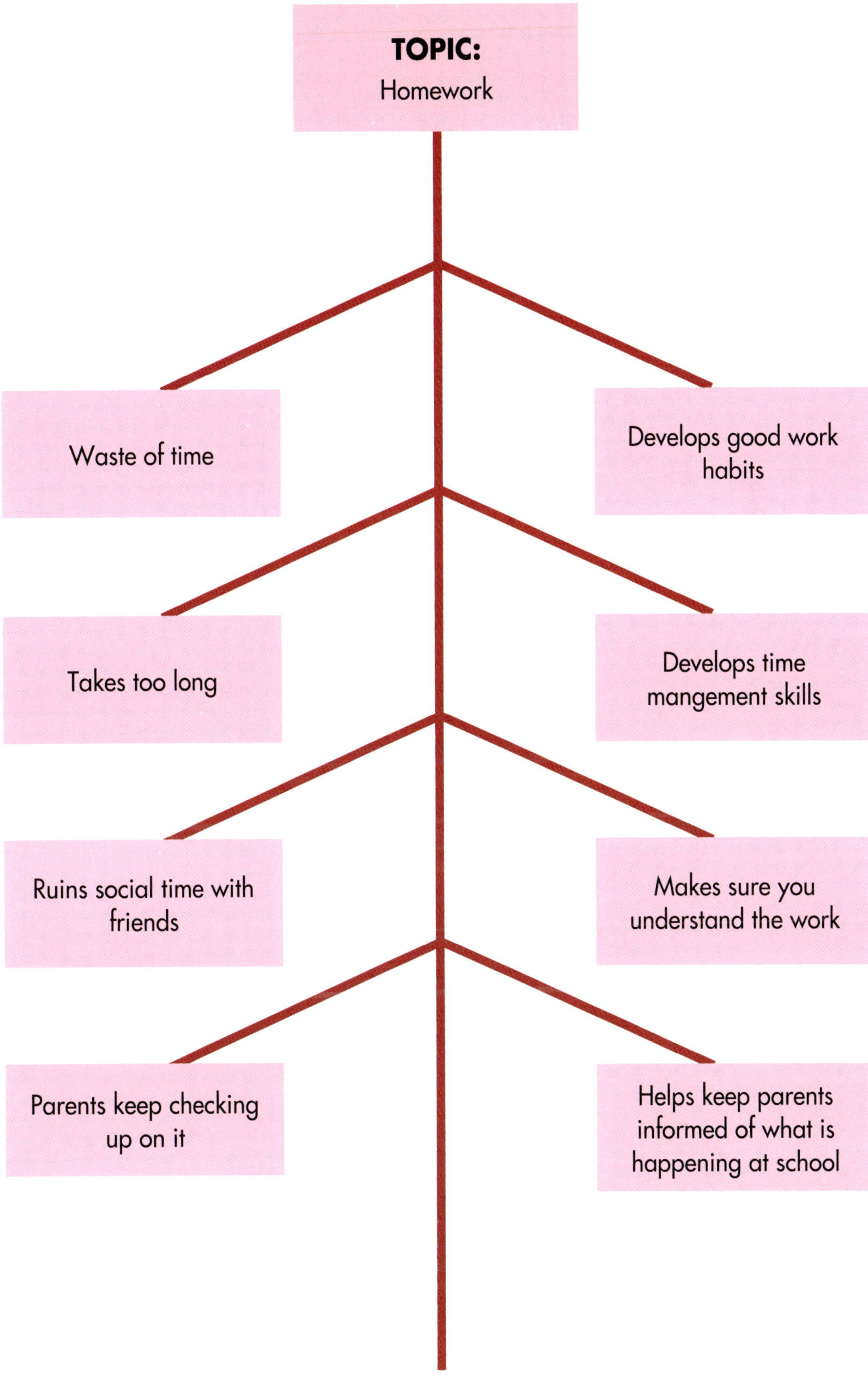

Tree diagram *(useful for recounts, reviews, biographies, descriptions, letters to the editor)*

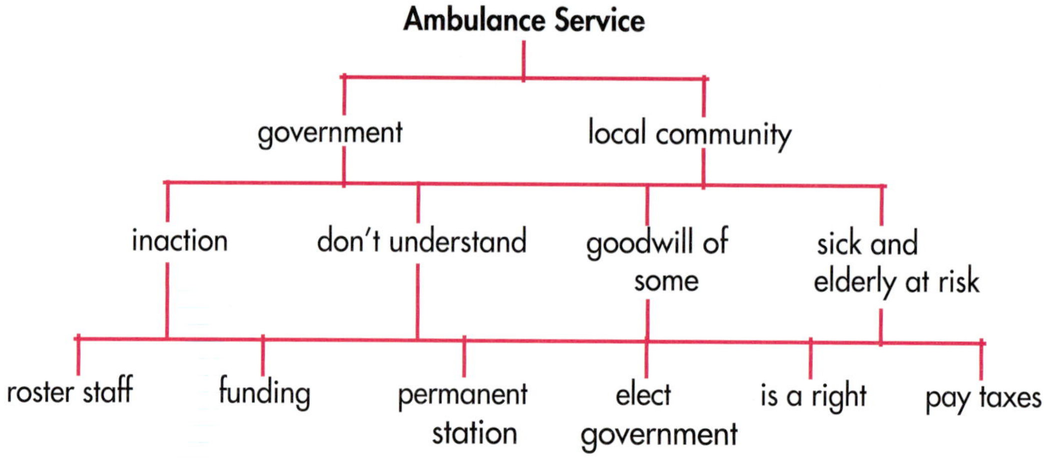

Survey grid *(useful for reviews, expositions, advertising, discussions)*

Blake's Writer's Guide – What do you think?

Questions	Did you find the format easy to use? Why?	What features of the book did you like best? Why?	Would you use the book? Why?
PERSON	**Response**	**Response**	**Response**
Leah	Yes. I liked the index so I could find stuff.	I liked the text samples, I can see what it should be like.	For sure. It has everything I need to know.
William	It was OK. There was lots in it.	My best thing was the editing tools. I need help doing that.	Maybe. My mum helps me a lot too.
Phoebe	Yeah because there wasn't too much on each page.	The planning organisers were good. Makes it easier to get started.	Yes I will. If I get stuck, I can look up what I need.
Ahmed	Sort of. It could have had more about web publishing.	I liked the NAPLAN stuff because I have to do it next year.	Yep because it tells me things I didn't know.
Hannah	I liked it a lot. The coloured boxes made it easy to see what you were looking for.	It was all good.	All the time! The tool box will help me heaps.

Star writing *(useful for all written text types)*

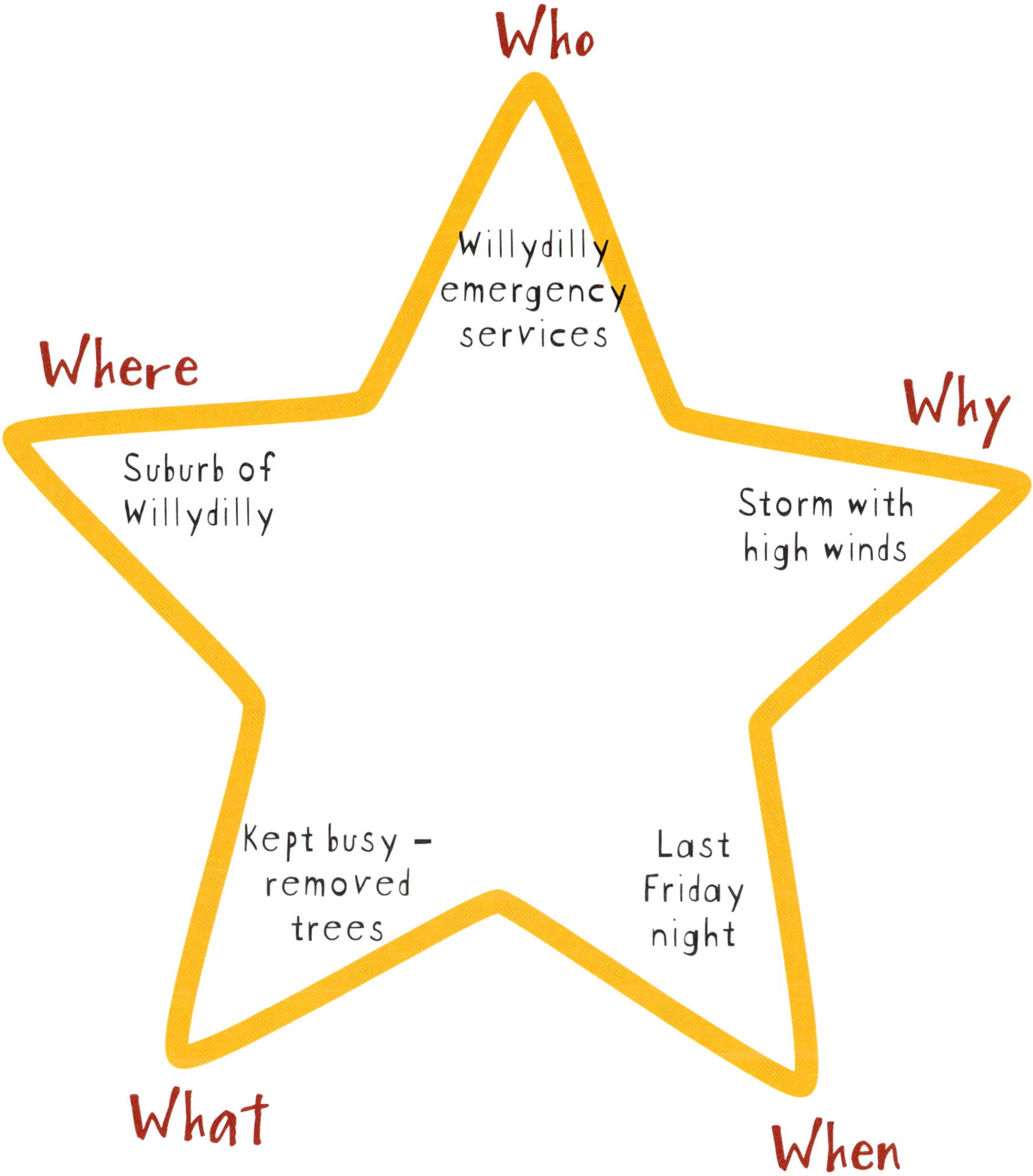

ESTABLISHING A SETTING

Describe the timeframe and setting of the story

If you are writing an imaginary text, creating a setting for your story is really important. If your setting is weak, it is like watching a movie with no background – just a blank wall. Here are some strategies you can use to create interesting and effective story settings.

- **Describe the timeframe that the story happens in.**
  There was a hush over the moonlit clearing. It was almost midnight and most of the creatures had settled down for the night.
- **Describe the appearance of the setting.**
  The noise was deafening as the crowd jostled each other to get a better view. Every now and then, smells of greasy hot dogs and buttery popcorn wafted through the stands, making mouths water.
- **Describe the setting by leaving out some information.**
  We turned the corner into Wentworth Street as we usually did this time of the morning. But today it felt different. There wasn't the usual hum of engines and rattle of bicycle chains. Today it was empty. Where was the traffic?
- **Describe the setting from a character's point of view.**
  I sat down in the cool shade of the old bakery awning, thankful for the relief from the scorching sun above. You certainly didn't get weather as hot as this back home.

Describe the setting from a character's point of view

Remember, when describing your setting make sure you know it well enough so you can bring it to life for the reader. If you believe it, so will they.

If you are writing a story with an historical background, you need to make sure that the setting is accurate for the time period. If it is science fiction, or a future time, make sure the setting is different from the present.

CREATING CHARACTERS

Creating believable characters is very important when writing imaginary texts, particularly narratives. It can also become important in argumentative texts when you have to take on the role of a character using first person.

The way to make characters seem real to the audience is to use a combination of **description, dialogue, action** and **interaction** with other characters.

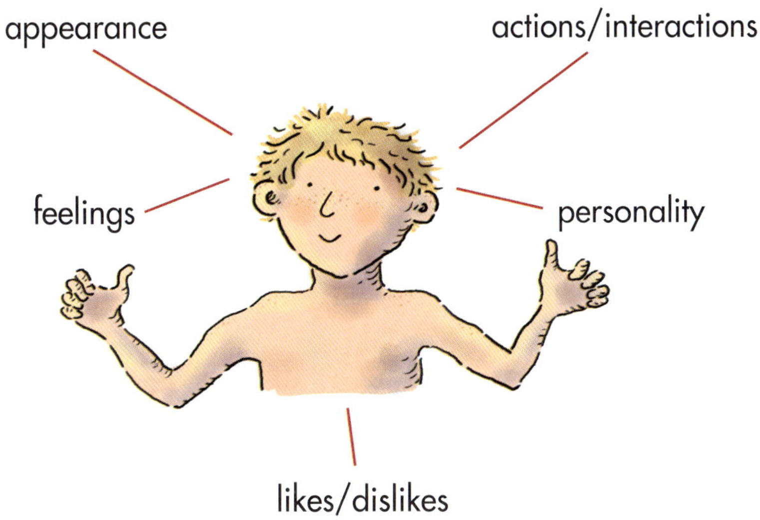

Description:

Here you need to remember to describe:

- the physical **appearance** of a character, eg blonde hair, blue eyes, bulging muscles, freckles
- the **personality** of the character, eg friendly and bubbly, withdrawn and silent, angry and confrontational
- the personal **history** of the character, eg had been alone for many long years; had recently lost his/her parents in a car accident; had a troublesome relationship with his/her big sister.

Through the words they use, the audience can learn a lot about the type of character they are.

Dialogue:

In your story, the characters will talk to each other, or sometimes they will even talk to themselves as they 'think out loud'. Through the words they use and how you describe their speech the audience can learn a lot about the type of character they are.

- *"Who . . . wh . . . who is it?" he enquired timidly.*

The reader knows the state of mind of the character because of the stammering and the use of the adverb 'timidly'.

- *"If you want our tails to decorate your hat, you'll have to come and get them!" they called to the pig.*

The reader can tell that the wolves are feeling brave. They are not stammering anymore and are speaking more forcefully than earlier in the story.

Then he tiptoed over and opened the window just a crack.

Action:

How a character behaves gives the reader a better understanding of who they are. It helps to make them more 'real', someone the audience can identify with.

- *Quietly he hopped out of bed and put on his slippers (he didn't want to wake up mum). Then he tiptoed over and opened the window just a crack.*

Here, Ben shows that he is a careful boy who knows the rules of not getting out of bed. We know that he doesn't want to get in trouble by waking his mother. His actions tell the reader that he is not brash and impulsive, but curious and inquisitive.

Interaction:

A character's relationship with others tells the audience a lot about them.

- *They huddled together in the kitchen and worked out a cunning plan.*

The little wolves get on well and care about each other. They will face any problems together and not by trying to be a hero alone.

DRAFTING

Step 2

Now you have done your research and you have the information you need. It's time to put it all together.

An effective opening encourages people to keep reading

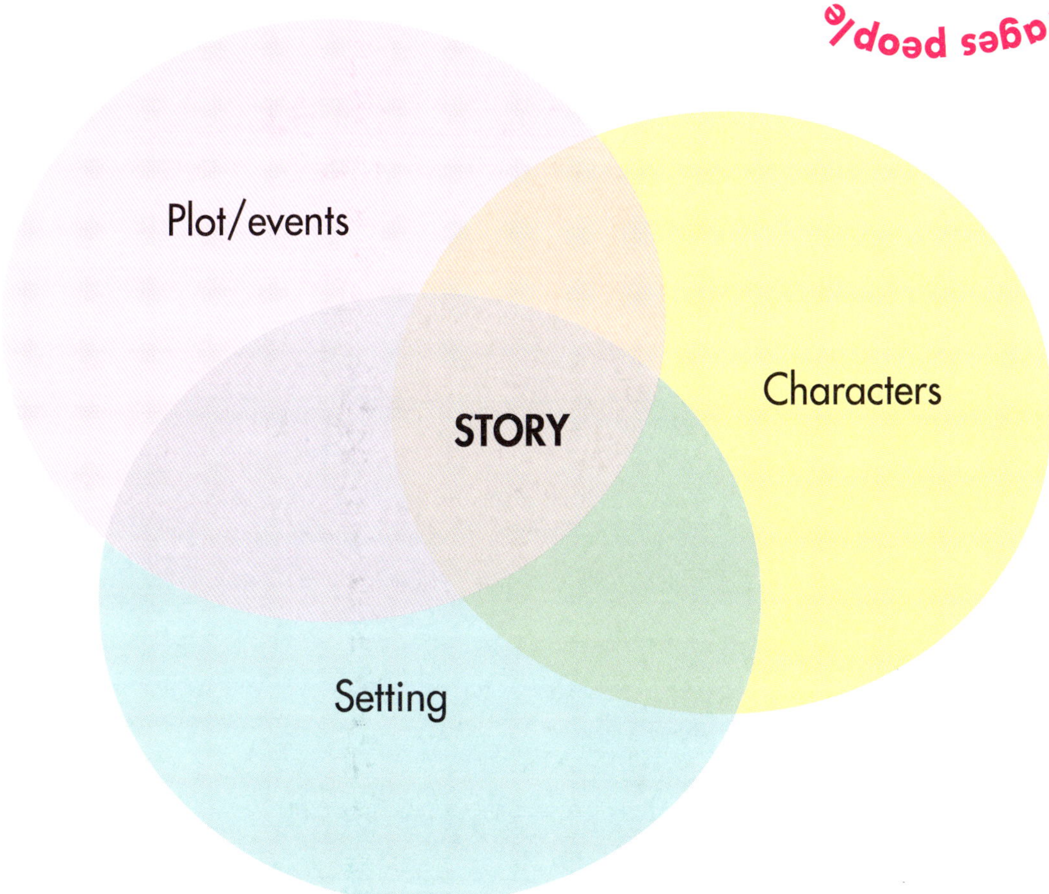

The hardest part of writing for most authors is getting started. Once you have the first couple of sentences or the introductory paragraph, you can follow your plan and the writing seems to flow. If you have an effective opening to your writing, your audience is encouraged to continue reading. However, if your beginning is boring, lacks direction or is off the topic, the audience may not bother reading much more. So, the question is: How to make a good start?

GOOD BEGINNINGS FOR IMAGINATIVE TEXTS*

An interesting question can take the reader straight into the action.

- Use dialogue to introduce the reader to the characters in a very personal way.
  ". . . and so Flobot and Marty Martian lived happily ever after," finished Mum.
  "Read it again!" Ben cried excitedly.
- Use an interesting sentence that takes the reader straight into the action.
  It was the most amazing feeling that Ben had ever experienced in his whole life.
- Use a question to involve the reader actively in the story.
  What was Ben going to do?
  What would you do?
- Use an exclamation to startle the reader.
  An alien spaceship had just landed on his roof!
- Use a description to create clear images of the setting in the mind of the reader.
  The silvery moonlight shone like a tractor beam, lighting up the landing strip of Ben's roof.
  The nearby trees began to swish and sway with the oncoming rush of wind.
- Introduce the main character so the reader can identify with him or her.
  Ben was an unusual boy with a love of the extraterrestrial.
- Use flashbacks to create a sense of intrigue. Instead of telling a story in chronological order, try starting at the end and then retell the events that led up to that point in the story.

  It had been the most amazing night of Ben's life. He could hardly believe all that he had been through in the past two and a half hours.

  The adventure had started when he was woken by a strange noise coming from outside his bedroom window.

Introduce the main character so the reader can identify with him or her.

**See pp. 61,77 for examples of imaginative texts*

GOOD BEGINNINGS FOR INFORMATIVE TEXTS*

Informative texts need to make sure that they orientate the reader by giving important background information that answers:

- **who?**
- **where?**
- **when?**
- **why?**

Using a variety of different paragraph and sentence starters helps make sure that the audience finds your writing interesting and enjoyable to read.

You can start whole texts, paragraphs or sentences by using:

❖ adverbial phrases or clauses
After a quick snack...
As the water rushed away...
When we arrived...

❖ passive voice
The equipment was placed...

❖ a complex noun group followed by an interesting verb
A tattered scrap of cloth enveloped...

❖ a rhetorical question
Have you ever wondered what makes a volcano erupt?

❖ a present participle
Leaping to great heights...

❖ a clear and short topic statement
A fax machine sends and receives electronic copies of printed material using telephone lines.

❖ a sentence that appeals directly to the audience
Think of a volcano as a pimple on your face, the slightest pressure and it can explode.

❖ a sentence that helps the audience understand the order of events
To understand how lightning occurs, first you need to know about how storms are created.

*See pp. 78,98 for examples of informative texts

Use a variety of different paragraph and sentence starters to make your writing interesting.

Think of a volcano as a pimple on your face...

GOOD BEGINNINGS FOR PERSUASIVE TEXTS*

You can grab a reader's attention by using a rhetorical question.

Persuasive or argumentative texts need to make a point, or persuade the audience to take a particular point of view. As such, their introductions need to be clear and simply summarise the message. They may be bold, inspiring or controversial, demanding that the audience continue reading.

Why on earth would anyone want to smoke?

Some interesting ways to grab a reader's attention in persuasive texts are:

- use a headline with powerful language
  Dream Team Slam Dunk Opponents
  Government Fails Crucial Test
- use a catchy or rhyming slogan
  Click clack front and back
- use a rhetorical question
  Why on earth would anyone want to smoke?
- use an endorsement
  Voted 'Best New Day-Spa' in TeenRulz magazine January 2009
- use emotive language aimed directly at the reader
  Quite clearly you wouldn't stoop so low as to agree with such flimsy arguments.
- use the personal pronoun 'we'
  We believe that it is vitally important to stop the hunting of whales in the South Pacific Ocean.
- use passive voice
  The building of a new high-rise apartment block will bring major traffic congestion and pollution issues to an already overcrowded suburb.
- a short and clear topic statement
  Each year countless animal species are added to the world's critically endangered list.

*See pp. 99,113 for examples of persuasive/argumentative texts

USING SPEECH IN WRITING

Often writers communicate ideas, events and emotions through the words of a character. To do this, they need to relay the character's speech effectively to the reader.

There are two types of speech in writing.

It is a good idea to use some direct speech and some reported speech, because its gives your writing variety and makes it more interesting.

1. Direct speech

This is where an author writes the exact words spoken by a character. It gives readers a better insight into the personality of the character, but it can sometimes slow down the pace of the action. Direct speech has special punctuation that must be used.

- At the start of a sentence:
  "Little wolves, let me in," called the pig.

A comma is used at the end of the speech because it is not the end of the written sentence.

- At the end of a sentence:
  The pig called, "Little wolves, let me in."

A comma is used to separate the narrative from the speech and the speech ends in a full stop because it is the end of the written sentence.

- Speech interrupted by text:
  "Little wolves," called the pig, "let me in."

A comma is used to separate the speech parts from the narrative.

Remember that punctuation markers (? , ! .) need to go inside the speech marks.

2. Reported speech

This is where an author writes about what was said by another person or character. They do not use the exact words spoken. Reported speech is handy when you want to summarise details and compare what is said with what is thought or acted upon.

Peter said that he would tell Miss Taylor that the dog had eaten his homework.

Reported speech can also be used in informative and argumentative texts to talk about what other people have said. It helps give your arguments credibility, and persuades others to believe in them.

When writing, particularly narratives, it is a good idea to use some direct speech and some reported speech, because its gives your writing variety and makes it more interesting.

SEQUENCING IDEAS

Ideas or events need to flow from one to the other so the reader can make sense of the meaning or the message.

It doesn't matter whether your writing is a narrative, procedure, explanation, discussion, letter or exposition, the ideas or events need to flow from one to the other so the reader can make sense of the meaning or the message.

This is where the use of **conjunctions** (to join parts of the same sentence) and **connectives** (to link ideas and events in different sentences) are so important.

Imaginative texts (See pp. 61,77)

In an imaginary text such as a narrative, the sequence of events is shown chronologically through the use of time adverbials.

Words

next	afterwards
later	eventually
then	finally
suddenly	

Phrases

A long time ago
Once upon a time
As the stranger turned away
Upon the return of the group
When I woke up
While the boys were shopping

Changing the way you use time adverbials can also help to make your writing more interesting, or it can serve to emphasise a particular part of the sentence. For example:

- The students played on the oval **while** the teachers ate lunch in the staffroom.
- **While** the teachers ate lunch in the staffroom, the students played on the oval.

Informative texts (See pp. 78,98)

In informative texts such as information reports or explanations, conjunctions and connectives are used to join different parts of your writing that are often separated by paragraphs.

Some connectives sequence events and ideas through time:

- Later on
- After that
- Next
- Finally
- Towards the end
- To begin with

Some connectives describe cause and effect relationships:

- if
- therefore
- because of this
- since
- consequently

Some connectives can introduce an interesting or surprising idea or condition:

- However
- Although
- Otherwise
- Despite

Remember: when you use a conjunction or a connective, you may also need to use a comma to separate clauses in your writing.

Persuasive texts (See pp. 99,113)

In these types of texts, such as letters to the editor, expositions and discussions, conjunctions and connectives serve a slightly different purpose to those used in other text types.

They are still used to sequence time:

- first
- once
- eventually
- previously

They are used to add an idea or argument:

- also
- as well as
- in addition to
- similarly

They are used to present an opposite idea or argument:

- but
- however
- on the other hand
- although

They are used to conclude the writing:

- in conclusion
- in short
- with regard to

They are used to give examples to support ideas and arguments:

- since
- for example
- because
- nevertheless

LOCATING MAIN IDEAS AND SUPPORTING DETAILS

When writing informative or argumentative texts, you need to make sure that each paragraph has a main idea accompanied by some supporting evidence or details, usually in separate sentences within the paragraph.

Main idea

A queen bee will begin laying eggs 10 days after mating. Each egg will be placed in a cell in the comb (inside the hive). She will lay about 3000 eggs a day for the rest of her life, about 2 years, and she will never leave the hive.

Supporting details

The main idea is also sometimes known as a topic sentence.

FACT AND OPINION

The difference between fact and opinion is very important when you are writing informative and persuasive texts. Imaginative texts, because they are created in the imagination of the writer, do not have to worry too much about fact and opinion.

Facts can be PROVED.
'Earth is the 3rd planet from the sun.'

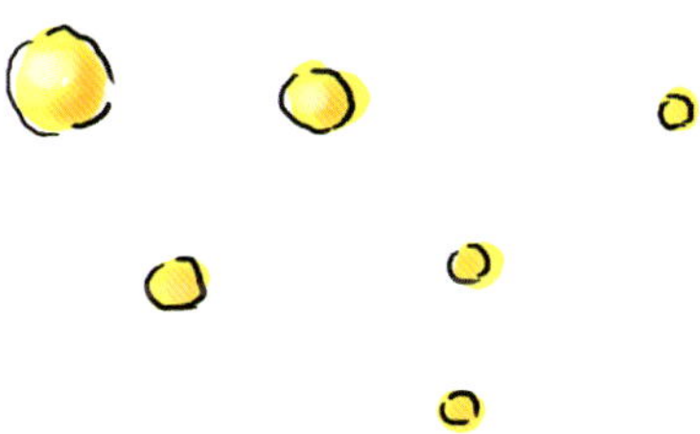

Informative texts are supposed to be based on fact rather than opinion. As a reader, you expect texts such as procedures, reports and recounts to give you true details, not something made up. So it is important to make sure your research is accurate before writing informative texts.

Opinions cannot be proved.
'My dog is the best pet in the world'.

Persuasive or argumentative texts are often a mixture of fact and opinion. If a writer can give some facts to support their opinions, it provides their text with **credibility**, as it shows that the writer knows about the topic.

Opinions cannot be proved. They are a BELIEF or THOUGHT.

Sometimes good writers can disguise opinion as fact. This is a useful tool as it can help persuade the reader into believing the opinion of the writer. Such tools are often found in advertising where the reader is led to believe something, but is not given real proof. For example: *The Little Boring Day Spa is thought by many to be the best in the country.*

BIAS

Bias is often found in argumentative writing, although reading audiences also have to be aware of it in informative writing such as biographies and news articles. Bias is the preference for or the dislike of something. It does not need to have a logical explanation. It is the opinion of the author.

The beach was a sunlit picture as golden rays of light sparkled like diamonds on the crests of the waves. Dozens of people relaxed at the water's edge enjoying the fresh salty spray.	The beach was hot and sultry and the merciless sun beat down on the pumping surf. Dozens of people skirted the water's edge, avoiding the salty sea spray.

Comparing these two accounts of the same scene, the text on the left has a favourable bias *(sparkled like diamonds, relaxed, enjoying)*, while the text on the right has an unfavourable bias *(hot, merciless, avoiding).*

When reading a text, the audience can only read the words the author wrote; they cannot question them or see into their thoughts and beliefs.

GOOD ENDINGS FOR IMAGINATIVE TEXTS*

The ending of a story is the last chance a writer has to leave a lasting impression on their audience.
The ending of a story needs to either solve the complication, identify what the characters have learnt or how they have changed, or encourage the audience to want to read the next story in the series, or other books by the same author.

For a successful ending try subverting or overturning the usual 'happily ever after' idea

Traditional narratives tend to end with 'happily ever after' **scenarios** where the Prince and Princess get married, or the evil dragon is slain. Other common narratives end with the victory of the main character over the forces of nature, or the criminal is found out. Some imaginative texts end with a moral or message of warning for readers about their own behaviour.

To make the ending of your imaginative text successful, try subverting or overturning the usual 'happily ever after' idea. Maybe the Princess turns out to be an ogre in disguise (as in the movie *Shrek*), or perhaps the frog turns into a Prince, but the Princess chooses to marry the palace gardener instead!

**See pp. 61,77 for examples of imaginative texts*

Other effective ways to end a story include:

- **questions:** I could almost feel the creature's musty breath on my neck as I ran towards the doorway. Would I be safe on the other side?
- **ellipses:** Calmly I made my way out of the forest, thinking about how lucky I had been to survive. Then I heard a noise behind me. I turned around and …
- **exclamation marks:** What a day! How lucky I was!
- **brackets:** After all that, the teams left the oval. The Blairmont Rangers were determined to win the Premiership once again (but there was still one team standing in their way).

GOOD ENDINGS FOR INFORMATIVE AND ARGUMENTATIVE TEXTS*

A good strong ending is one that serves to summarise the main points and leave a lasting impression on the reader.

POOR ENDING	GOOD ENDING
So that is why we need an ambulance service in Dunbeena.	Access to adequate emergency services is a right for all residents. You don't have to be Einstein to work out what should be done!

Some points to remember for ending factual texts:

- summarise what happened and why
- restate your point of view with key examples
- appeal to the audience directly by asking a question.

*See pp. 78,98 for examples of informative texts
See pp. 99,113 for examples of argumentative texts

REVISING Step 3

As a writer, rereading and revising your work is very important. This is the step in the writing process where you check and try to improve your text.

Read your writing aloud to a friend and ask for feedback

You will find the task of revising made easier if you read your writing aloud to a friend. Your friend can then help you by giving feedback on what parts of your writing they liked and how they think you could make it better. It is also a good idea to give yourself some time between the steps of drafting and revising, so that you read the text with fresh eyes.

You need to look at:

- the text as a whole (its structure and organisation)
- each paragraph (its main idea and supporting information)
- each sentence (its meaning and structure)
- each word (its strength and meaning)

This is the step in the writing process where you check and try to improve your text.

Also remember that spelling and punctuation are not very important in the revising stage. They are dealt with in step 4 (editing).

REVISING IMAGINATIVE TEXTS (See pp. 61,77)

Imaginative texts focus on entertaining the reader, thrilling them, scaring them and intriguing them. As such, the key to revising imaginative texts is looking at sentence structure and word usage, as well as strong starts and effective endings.

Revision Frame for Imaginative Texts

Criteria	Always	Some	Rarely	Ideas for revision
1. Title – is it interesting? Does it introduce the topic?				
2. Introduction – is it strong? Does it grab reader interest?				
3. Sentences – is there variety? Do they flow? Are they in order?				
4. Words – is there variety? Effective noun groups? Vibrant verbs? Appropriate adverbs? Good connectives?				
5. Ending – is it satisfying? Does it make sense? Is it strong?				
6. Have I met the needs of the target audience?				
7. Have I achieved the purpose of entertaining?				
8. Is my format and structure going to appeal to the audience?				

REVISING INFORMATIVE TEXTS (See pp. 78,98)

Informative texts rely on accurate ideas and details. The revision of these texts means that you as the writer must focus on organisation and word choice.

Revision Frame for Informative Texts

Criteria	Always	Some	Rarely	Ideas for revision
1. Title – does it clearly identify the topic?				
2. Introduction – is it a general statement about the topic?				
3. Does each paragraph have a main idea?				
4. Does each paragraph give details to support the main idea?				
5. Do I use effective connectives to make the ideas flow?				
6. Do I use technical words appropriately?				
7. Have I organised my writing with headings and/or paragraphs?				
8. Do I use a variety of sentence structures?				
9. Have I used complex noun groups?				
10. Have I used interesting verbs and adverbs?				
11. Is my ending effective?				
12. Does my writing inform the reader?				
13. Have I referenced my work?				
14. Have I included an accurate glossary?				

REVISING PERSUASIVE TEXTS (See pp. 99,113)

Persuasive or argumentative texts rely on the writer persuading the audience to believe a particular point of view. As such, the revision of these texts involves looking at word choice, voice and fluency.

Revision Frame for Persuasive Texts

Criteria	Always	Some	Rarely	Ideas for revision
1. Title – does it ask a question? Does it grab attention?				
2. Introduction – does it state or define the topic? Does it give a point of view?				
3. Are the arguments presented in separate paragraphs?				
4. Does each paragraph have a main idea?				
5. Does each paragraph have examples or details that support the argument?				
6. Do the arguments and paragraphs flow?				
7. Have I used connectives well?				
8. Is my voice biased?				
9. Have I used emotional words?				
10. Have I used a variety of thinking verbs?				
11. Does the conclusion summarise key points? State point of view?				
12. Have I referenced my work?				

REVISING SENTENCES

Sentences in any form of writing should flow fluently through the reader's voice and mind. Short choppy sentences can make the details seem disjointed and not connected to the main idea.

Very long sentences, however, can lose a reader as they struggle to remember what happened at the beginning and trace the subject of the sentence.

Short choppy sentences

Draft sentence	My dog is Jessie. She is black. She is a Labrador. She likes to chew on bones. She also likes to dig holes.
Revised sentence	My dog Jessie is a black Labrador. She likes to chew on bones and dig holes.

Long boring sentences

Draft sentence	I like my friend Kayla who lives next door to me and has blonde hair because she is always nice to me and she helps look after me in the playground when I fall over and hurt myself.
Revised sentence	My friend Kayla has blonde hair and lives next door to me. I like her because she is always nice to me. Kayla helps me when I fall over and hurt myself in the playground.

REVISING WORD CHOICE

The words you choose to use in your writing are your main link with the audience. They communicate events, emotions and personalities, and they help create visual images of characters and settings in the mind of the reader. Good word choice is essential.

Nouns and noun groups

Draft sentence	The boys put their stuff in the room.
Revised sentence	The school football team put their equipment in the locker room.

The use of good nouns and noun groups makes your writing more interesting, and the reader has a better understanding of the topic.

Verbs and verb groups

Draft sentence	The bike went down the hill as the dog ran after it. "Oh no!" the rider said as he came to a stop at the bottom.
Revised sentence	The bike hurtled wildly down the hill as the dog madly chased after it. "Oh no!" the rider cried as he skidded to a stop at the bottom.

REVISING CONJUNCTIONS AND CONNECTIVES

These are words that help link parts of sentences together, or link ideas in different sentences together, so that the writing can 'flow' and makes sense as a whole text.

Including conjunctions

Draft sentence	The three little wolves built a raging fire under the chimney. They spent the next couple of days feasting on smoked bacon.
Revised sentence	The three little wolves built a raging fire under the chimney **and** spent the next couple of days feasting on smoked bacon.

Removing conjunctions

Draft sentence	This made him very angry indeed **and so** the big bad pig climbed up onto the roof **and** stuffed himself in the chimney **and** he was too fat to fit **and he** got stuck
Revised sentence	This made him very angry indeed. **So** the big bad pig climbed up onto the roof **and** stuffed himself into the chimney. **But** he was too fat to fit **and** he got stuck.

Including connectives

Draft sentence	Mankind has been fascinated by what lay beyond Earth. It wasn't until 1971 that Mariner 9 observed canyons and channels on Mars. In 1976 two Viking spacecraft landed on Mars. In 1995 NASA sent out the Mars Pathfinder.
Revised sentence	**Ever since recorded history began**, mankind has been fascinated by what lay beyond Earth. **Yet** it wasn't until 1971 that Mariner 9 observed canyons and channels on Mars. **Several years later**, in 1976 two Viking spacecraft landed on Mars. **Two decades later**, in 1995, NASA sent out the Mars Pathfinder.

Using a variety of connectives

Draft sentence	On the weekend I went to the park. **First** I went on the swings. **Then** I played in the sandpit. **Then** I slid down the slippery dip. **Then** I had a picnic lunch. **Finally** I went home.
Revised sentence	On the weekend I went to the park. **When I got there** I went on the swings. **Then** I played in the sandpit before sliding down the slippery dip. **Later in the afternoon** I went home.

REVISING PARAGRAPHS

Often when you start drafting a piece of writing, you concentrate on getting down your ideas and you forget to put it in paragraphs. Once the draft is finished and you are at the revision stage, this is the time when you need to check to make sure that you have paragraphs.

A paragraph can be a single sentence, but it is usually made up of several sentences about a particular idea or topic. Paragraphs help readers follow a long story or text. They are shown by either indenting the first line, as this paragraph has been, or by using a line break.

Paragraphs that are too long can be boring and lose the reader, while paragraphs that are too short seem jerky. Sometimes, however, short paragraphs can be used to create a sense of excitement and drama.

Remember when you are revising your paragraphs to make sure that they do not all start the same way and that you have used different and interesting connectives to make your writing flow.

You need to start a new paragraph when:

- there is a new event in the plot (After lunch they went for a walk . . .)
- there is a new time period (The next day . . .)
- the setting has changed (Once back in New York . . .)
- there is a new piece of information (As well as this, the labrador has . . .)
- a new character is speaking ("That will be fine," replied Mum.)
- a new argument or idea is presented (Another reason why . . .)
- an opposite point of view is presented (However, not everyone will agree with . . .)

Step 4

PROOFREADING AND EDITING

Punctuation varies according to the type of sentence

This is the final chance you have to fix up any mistakes, particularly in the areas of spelling and punctuation.

For more details on correct spelling strategies please refer to *Blake's Spelling Guide*.

PUNCTUATING SENTENCES

Different types of sentences require different types of punctuation.

- **Statement** – requires a capital letter to start and a full stop at the end.
  The dog ran across the street.
  (tells the reader something)
- **Question** – requires a capital letter to start and a question mark at the end.
  What time will the game start?
  (asks something)
- **Exclamation** – requires a capital letter to start and an exclamation mark at the end.
  I couldn't believe my eyes when I saw it!
  (gives a feeling of surprise, anger or excitement)
- **Command** – requires a capital letter to start and a full stop at the end.
  Give me the toothpaste.
  (tells someone what to do)

For punctuation rules for speech, please refer to the section on Direct Speech p.27.

PUNCTUATING WITH COMMAS

A comma is used to separate words or parts of sentences to help the reader understand the meaning.

- commas in a list (to separate three or more items)
  At the shop I bought oranges, apples, bananas and pears.
- commas in adverbial phrases and clauses (used to describe the verb in the sentence)
  Finally, Sarah could rest.
- commas to act as brackets (to contain specific information)
  Ali, who was the eldest, led the way.
- commas to separate main clauses and dependent clauses
  Looking around carefully, Jarred crept towards the fence.

At the shop I bought oranges, apples, bananas and pears.

PUNCTUATING WITH APOSTROPHES

An apostrophe can be used to show missing letters in a contraction or the possession of an object by a character.

- contractions
  do not = don't *can not = can't*
  they are = they're *she will = she'll*
- possession (singular owner)
  my mum's car *the dog's breakfast*
  Benji's school book
- possession (plural owner)
  the bones of the dogs = the dogs' bones
  the books of the girls = the girls' books

ADVANCED PUNCTUATION MARKS

- A **colon (:)** is used to introduce information such as a list or an explanation.
  The children had prepared well: hats, sun block and towels were all packed.
- A **semicolon (;)** is used instead of a conjunction to separate clauses in a sentence.
  The house was hidden in the mist; it looked eerie and forbidden.
- **Dashes (–)** are used to introduce a sudden surprise or dramatic ending, or to show an interruption in speech.
  The children dragged themselves home – soaking wet but safe.
  "And as the horses round the bend, Lucky Lady – no, Joyful Landing is in the lead!"
- **Brackets ( )** are used to include extra information.
  The car (with a top speed of 145 km/h) raced around the track.
- **Bullet points (•)** are used for listing key points of information or ideas. They are often found in informative texts such as reports.

If the points are single words or short phrases, punctuate like this:

A good writer has the following characteristics:

- *reads a lot*
- *reads widely*
- *uses interesting words.*

If the points are longer statements, but not separate sentences, punctuate with semicolons like this:

Students in Years 5 and 6 reported that:

- *over half of them had been bullied;*
- *more than 90% of the bullying had been resolved;*
- *they were nervous about going to high school.*

If the points are separate sentences, end each with a full stop like this:

Year 5 and 6 students were surveyed and the results are as follows:

- *The most popular subject was Creative Arts.*
- *The least popular subject was Mathematics.*
- *More than 98% of the students enjoyed being at school.*

(Univeristy of Bristol, 2008)

USING PROOFREADING MARKS

When you are editing your writing, it helps if you use commonly understood proofreading marks so that other people know what you mean.

Proofreading marks

^	Insert
sp	Spelling mistake
⊙	Add a full stop
[	Start a new paragraph
	Delete
#	Put in a space
“ ” with ∨ ∨	Put in speech marks

Look at this proofreading example

"Come on Mum!" I yelled. But still she couldn't here me. After waiting a few more minutes, I decided to go outside by miself. It was a warm and sunny day and the flowers were just starting to blossom the garden. I loved this time of the year. Mum! I called again. This time she ansered. "I'll just be a minute Charlie." Then she appeared at the doorway holding my hat and sunnies in her hand

Step 5

PUBLISHING

Experienced authors don't publish everything they write

When you publish your writing, you are opening it up to a public audience. Because of this, it needs to be your best work – completed, revised and edited.

Other people don't like reading material with lots of errors, or that doesn't make sense.

It is important to remember that even very experienced authors do not publish everything they write. It all depends upon the purpose for the writing, the intended audience and whether or not the author actually likes what they have written.

Published writing needs:

- to be written clearly
- to have a strong beginning and ending
- to have a clear purpose
- to be visually appealing
- to be willingly shared by the author.

PUBLISHING FORMATS

You can choose to publish your writing in a variety of different ways that suit both your own personal style, as well as the needs of your chosen audience. If you are publishing a letter to the editor, for example, a comic strip format would not be appropriate.

Below are some ways in which you may choose to publish your writing:

- make a picture book
- make a poster
- record a reading of your story onto a tape, CD or MP3
- make a brochure
- make a class magazine or newspaper
- post your story on a class or school website
- make a comic strip
- email it to a friend or relative
- make an electronic story on the computer using programs such as PowerPoint
- perform your story as a reader's theatre
- record your performance on video and publish using computer programs such as Story Maker.

USING A COMPUTER TO HELP PUBLISH

Nowadays there are many different ways to use a computer to help you publish a text.

There is the standard word processing – or typing.

Use different fonts or writing styles to make headings and labels stand out.

Freehand MISTER FRISKY STENCIL

Chalkboard Typewriter

Use different font sizes.

Size 10 size 14 Size 20 Size 36

Use bold (Ctrl B), italic (Ctrl I) or underline (Ctrl U) tools (also found on tool bar).

Normal **Bold** *Italic* Underline

Use different coloured text to make your writing appealing and to separate sections as I have done on this page.

You can also use the highlighter tool next to the font colour icon to highlight words for a glossary or important steps.

Also look at the design or layout of your work on the page.

You can have your text starting at the left margin and working across to the right.

You can have your text orientated to the centre of the page for each line. Or perhaps just for a heading.

You can start your writing from the right hand side of the page. This layout is not used very often.

MORE CREATIVE WAYS TO USE A COMPUTER

Using programs such as PowerPoint, you can create a slide show of information for a report, a life cycle for an explanation or pages of a story with illustrations for a narrative. You can also use Microsoft Publisher to create letters, brochures and pamphlets. There are many similar programs that can also create computer-designed stories. Two you could try are Comic Life (http://plasq.com/comiclife-win) and Story Maker (http://www.britishcouncil.org/kids-writing-storymaker.htm)

Using PowerPoint

Once you have your draft text, open a new PowerPoint document and right click the mouse to pop up a menu. On the menu choose 'Slide design'. From here you can choose different backgrounds and colours for your pages. They can be the same if you choose the option 'Apply to all', or each slide can have a different background design.

Use the 'Insert' icon on the toolbar to insert text boxes for your writing. Type in as you normally would for any word processing, choosing your own colours, fonts and sizes. On the text box is a green ball. If you click on it, it will rotate the box to the left or the right to make your layout more interesting. Use the fill and line tools in your drawing toolbar to colour in the boxes and lines.

Again, use the 'Insert' icon to add pictures to your page(s). You can search for a clip art picture or get one from a file of your own photos. When you have inserted your picture, right click on it and choose 'Custom animation' from the pop up menu. Here you can add movement to the picture.

The 'Insert' icon menu can also be used to add tables, charts, graphs and diagrams such as flow charts to your text. This tool is very useful when publishing informative or argumentative texts.

Once you have typed in all your text and added appropriate visual effects, now it is time to add transitions, or movements, between each slide in the slideshow. Right click the mouse and select the menu option of 'Slide transition'. Experiment with the different styles and speeds and select the ones you want. It makes it easier if you select the 'Automatically after' option.

Now you are done! Push the F5 button on the keyboard to see your finished slide show.

Saving your work

This is important to do, no matter what computer-generated format you have used. Saving a PowerPoint slide show, a Publisher document or a word processing document follows the same process.

Saving your work

- Go to the File menu and click **Save**, or **Save as**.
- Look at the **Save in** box and select the file or folder where you want the work to be saved, eg *My work, Desktop*.
- At the bottom, go to the box titled **File name**.
- Type in the name of your piece of work, eg *The Three Little Wolves*.
- Now click on the **Save** icon at the bottom of the **Save** menu box.

TRAITS OF GOOD WRITING

Using a variety of words makes your writing more interesting

Good writing will feature all of the following traits, but how they are displayed will differ according to the text type used and the intended purpose and audience.

1. Ideas and details

These need to be clearly stated and focused on the specific topic. It needs to make sense at a whole text level, at a paragraph level and at a sentence level.

2. Organisation

Each text type has a specific organisational structure that should be followed so that ideas, information and events are sequenced in an easily understood way. Through the use of headings and subheadings and paragraphs, the reader should easily be able to follow the connections and changes within a text.

3. Voice

Good writing uses appropriate voice. The writer should appear to be informed about their subject matter – not necessarily an 'expert', but aware of the key facts and details. The writer should be aware of the audience they are writing for and whether they need to use formal or informal language, active or passive voice. You write for your intended audience.

4. Word choice

Using a variety of words makes your writing more interesting to read. The words used should reflect the needs of the audience. Do you need to use complex technical language when describing a bike to a four year old? Do you need to use casual slang when writing an information report for your teacher? It is important to widen your vocabulary, so remember to use a thesaurus.

5. Fluency

Sentences and paragraphs need to flow smoothly, to maintain a reader's understanding of the text. Poetry in particular relies on rhythm to make it easy and enjoyable to read. Remember to use a variety of interesting and appropriate conjunctions and connectives to help your ideas flow and be linked between sentences and paragraphs.

6. Conventions

These are the common conventions of spelling, punctuation, paragraphing and the use of grammar. As a reader, there is nothing worse than reading something that doesn't sound right or doesn't make sense. For example:

"We done went and did stuff today."

"We did some activities today."

TOOLS OF AN AUTHOR

To engage your audience you may look at 'sub-genre' styles

These tools will assist you greatly not only in your everyday writing, but also when completing your NAPLAN* assessments.

NAPLAN stands for 'National Assessment Program – Literacy and Numeracy' and is an Australia-wide test that covers reading, comprehension and grammar, mathematics and, of course, writing.

1. Engaging your audience

Throughout *Blake's Writer's Guide*, you have examined many different text types and some differing genre formats. To truly engage your audience you may also look at what are known as 'sub-genre styles'. You may have heard of movies being described as a 'chick flick', meaning they appeal mainly to a female audience. This is a sub-genre of a narrative. Others include black comedy and boys' own adventure.

You may also look at aspects of writing such as:

- **Subverting** expectations – where what happens is not what you thought would happen. For example in the movie *Shrek*, the princess turns out to be an ogre.
- Encourage the reader to reflect on their own actions and beliefs through the words and actions of one of your characters. Perhaps a character has been bullied and through their interactions and conversations, they work through their relationship problems with others – making the reader think of themselves in similar situations.
- Using **irony** in characters' speech to make it seem that the opposite of their words is actually true.

*This is not an officially endorsed publication of the NAPLAN program and is produced by Pascal Press independently of Australian Governments.

2. Using effective text structure

You know that the common structure for a narrative is:

Orientation → Complication → Resolution → Ending

But there are some more interesting ways to structure your narrative:

- **Parallel plots** – where you tell two stories at once. For example, the story of 'The Prince and the Pauper', where the narrative swaps between paragraphs or chapters to alternately tell the story of each child's life, until the two boys come together.

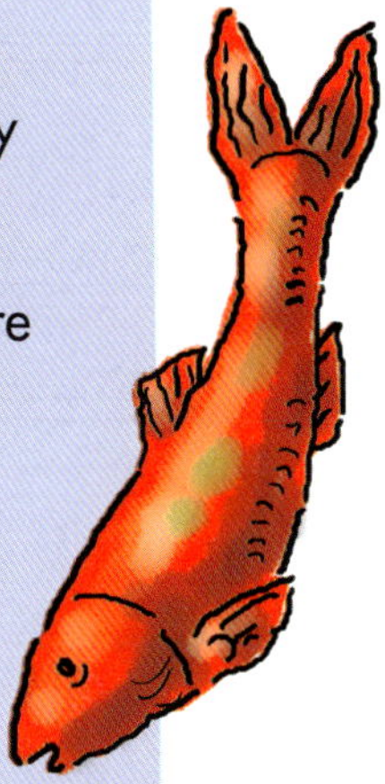

- **Red herring** – is used in mystery or detective narratives. It is where a clue or piece of information found is deliberately misleading. For example, the police are hunting a jewellery thief and at the crime scene they find a bus pass. They (and the reader) think it is connected to the thief, but in fact it has nothing to do with the crime.
- **Epiphany** – where after a series of events, or after a significant event, a character comes to a sudden realisation or idea.
- **Circular** – where the characters experience a series of events, involving trials and complications, but in the end they are back where they started from. For example: A group of children are lost in the forest; they encounter wild animals, fierce weather conditions, and an accident or injury; then, after days of wandering around, they find themselves back at the same campsite, but with an insight from the main character about their ordeal.
- **Anecdote** – where you start a narrative with an anecdote from one of the characters. Your story then continues along the normal narrative structure, examining more closely the events leading up to, or resulting from, the event in the anecdote. The narrative will usually end with a concluding comment or insight from the character.

3. Using interesting ideas

When you are choosing your topics or the subject matter for your writing, don't always go for the standard 'Once upon a time' story line.

- Try a mystery or 'whodunnit'.
- Use unusual topics or characters. For example: The Three Little Wolves and the Big Bad Pig.
- Add bits of our popular culture – such as fashion, music and dance styles (eg popping and krumping), and technology (eg characters who use their palm pilots to solve detective mysteries). Take care, though, that your choice of words won't 'date' your work too quickly.

VOCABULARY TOOLS

These are mainly found in imaginative texts such as narratives and poetry. However, they can also be used in informative texts such as reviews, reports and descriptions.

- **Alliteration** – a repeated consonant sound:
  Goofy Gavin grabbed a green grape
- **Assonance** – a repeated vowel sound:
  Hi ho, hi ho, it's off to work we go
- **Onomatopoeia** – the sound of a word mirrors its meaning:
  screech, clunk, whoosh
- **Simile** – the comparison of two things using 'like' or 'as':
  - common simile – *as red as a rose*
  - interesting simile – *the storm rolled in like a gigantic black glove smothering the city*
- **Metaphor** – the comparison of two things, saying one is the other:
  the wind is a howling wolf
- **Personification** – inanimate objects are given human characteristics:
  The coffee grinder ate its meal and then spat it out.
- **Colloquial** – informal language often used in character's speech:
  "Nah. I'm gonna get it tomorrow," replied Jake.

- **Figurative** – words that do not have the same meaning as their literal meaning:
  "You drive me up the wall," said Mum. (make me crazy)
  Our teacher told us to pull our socks up. (try harder)
  "Go jump in the lake!" yelled my little brother. (go away)

VERBS TO USE WITH SPEECH

Even though words are spoken or 'said' by a character, the way in which they are spoken, the tone and the manner, can be very different.

"Be quiet!" hissed the librarian.

"Be quiet!" hollered the Principal.

"Be quiet," soothed Mum.

"Be quiet," moaned his sister.

Here are some words you might find useful when using speech in your own writing.

USING A THESAURUS

Sometimes it can be difficult to think of different words when you are writing. A good tool to have is a thesaurus. This is a reference book like a dictionary that puts words into groups according to their meaning. It will have words of similar meaning (synonyms) and words with opposite meanings (antonyms). A thesaurus is organised alphabetically to help you find what you need.

Word → definition → grammar (N. = noun)

Wind [air in motion] – **N.** draught, puff, whiff, drift, stream, gust, blast, squall, gale, hurricane, tempest.

V. blow, waft, whistle, roar, breathe, belch, wheeze

Adj. windy, airy, breezy, gusty, blustery, tempestuous

Ant. still, airless, tranquil, stuffy, unventilated

Grammar (v. = verb) Grammar (Adj. = adjective) synonyms

(Ant. = antonyms)

(Roget P. M., 1972)

Instead of writing:

It was a very windy day. The strong wind was blowing the leaves around.

I could write:

It was a blustery day. The gusty breeze was blowing the leaves around.

USING A DICTIONARY

Having a dictionary close at hand while you write is a really good idea. Not only can it help you with correct spelling, but it can also help with making sure that the word you are using has the meaning that you want. It will also give alternative grammatical forms of the word to use in different ways. A dictionary is organised alphabetically to assist you in finding the word you need. Looking at each page, the first word on the page is in bold text at the top of the left hand column, while the last word on the page is in bold at the top of the right hand column.

456

ear **earmark**

ear – 1. the organ on the side of the head used for hearing. 2. top of a cereal plant such as corn that contains the grain or kernels.
earache – a sore ear.
eardrops – medicine used to cure earache.
earl – an English nobleman.
earldom – the title of an earl.
early – 1. arriving before expected. 2. happening in the near future.
early bird – a person who is early.
early warning – notice before an event happens.
earmark – to put aside for a special use.

word | pronunciation | grammatical form (verb) | meaning 1 | meaning 2

Inspect (in'spekt) *vb* 1. to look at closely, particularly for errors. 2. to examine officially (a document or military personnel etc). [from Latin inspicere] – inspectable adj.
– inspectingly adv. – inspection n.
– inspective adj.

Historical root of word

Different grammatical forms of the word
As an adverb, noun, adjective

(Collins English Dictionary, 1986)

PARTS OF A BOOK

There are two types of books: fiction and nonfiction

All books, no matter what their purpose or audience, follow a similar set of guidelines when it comes to their structure and layout. There are generally two types of books: fiction (imaginative) and nonfiction (factual).

Features of NONFICTION BOOKS

may have photographs, graphs and charts

index

glossary

bibliography or other references

headings and subheadings

Shared Features

cover with title and author

contents page

chapters

numbered pages

an information 'blurb' on the back cover

an imprint page inside the front cover

chapter titles

Features of FICTION BOOKS

may or may not have an illustrator

for younger readers may use colourful cartoon type illustrations

TEXT TYPES

WHAT ARE THE DIFFERENT TEXT TYPES?

All texts, both spoken and written, differ. What text type you use as a writer depends on what your purpose for writing is. Each text type has specific rules for how it is organised and what language is used.

There are three broad categories of text types:

Imaginative texts (fiction)

Examples of imaginative texts are narratives, fairytales, anecdotes, illustrated books, novels, plays and poetry. They use made-up characters and/or events and often involve the reader in a personal response. They can also involve magical or 'impossible' ideas such as talking animals and travel through time.

Informative texts (nonfiction)

These texts provide information in order to direct, inform or explain something to the reader. They usually try to be objective and not to take one side or one point of view over another. Informative texts use real people and real events. Examples of informative texts are recounts, reports, descriptions, explanations, biographies, news articles and procedures.

Persuasive or argumentative texts (nonfiction)

The purpose of an argumentative text is to persuade or to present two different sides of an issue. Your purpose as a writer is to get someone to think or act in a particular way. Persuasive texts involve subjective language where opinions and not just facts are used. Examples of argumentative texts are expositions, formal essays, letters to the editor, advertisements, reviews, interviews and discussions.

IMAGINATIVE texts use made-up characters and/or events

INFORMATIVE texts provide information to explain or direct

PERSUASIVE texts present two different sides of an issue

WHAT IS A GENRE?

A genre is a subgroup of a text type, like a category

Sometimes text types are called genres. However, genres are more than just different ways of structuring a piece of writing.

A genre is a subgroup of a text type, similar to a category. They usually share many features with the text type, with a few small differences such as format or settings. Below is a sample of some common genres:

	TEXT TYPE	GENRE
IMAGINATIVE	Narrative	• fairytale • folk tale • myths and legends • fable • fantasy • science fiction • historical fiction
	Poetry	• rhymes • acrostic • jingle • limericks • cinquain • haiku • free verse • song lyrics • catalogue
	Drama	• play scripts • improvisation
INFORMATIVE	Recount	• letter • journal • diary • autobiography • literary recount • factual recount
	Procedure	• recipe • directions • instructions • science experiment
	Report	• biography • current affairs • scientific report • documentary
	Explanation	• life cycle • mechanical handbook • medical journal
PERSUASIVE	Exposition	• current affairs • documentary • advertising • editorial • review
	Discussion	• current affairs • debate • documentary

IMAGINATIVE TEXTS | NARRATIVE

Purpose: A narrative is often referred to as a 'story'. They are usually fictitious, or 'made up'. They are written to entertain or amuse the reader.

Narratives have two main categories. One is traditional narratives, which include fairytales, folktales, fables, myths and legends. The other is modern fiction, which includes fantasy, mystery and science fiction.

Narratives can be found in picture books, short stories and novels. The story may be told by a narrator, or by the characters through their dialogue.

STRUCTURE CORE FEATURES	ADVANCED FEATURES
orientation – sets the scene by creating setting time and place, and introducing characters	set an 'atmosphere' – give details about character description and personality
	flashback
complication – there is a conflict or problem that affects the setting or the characters	a series of related or unrelated problems that reach a climax
resolution – the problem is solved	one or more of the problems may be unresolved or only partially resolved. The main character is changed by the experience.
ending – the normal pattern of life returns for the characters	makes explicit how the character/s have been changed and what has been learnt (moral)
	cliffhanger – unknown ending

LANGUAGE CORE FEATURES	ADVANCED FEATURES
nouns to name characters	extended noun groups
adjectives to describe setting and characters	adverbial phrases to describe action
action verbs	saying and thinking verbs
past tense	written in first person
dialogue for direct speech	personification
time connectives and conjunctions	similes and metaphors for description
written in third person	

Key features: Narrative – Science fiction genre

Read the example science fiction narrative below.
Can you find the key features of its structure and language? Use the features box to help you look.

There's an Alien in My Bedroom

"..... and so Flobot and Marty Martian lived happily ever after," finished Mum.

"Read it again!" Ben cried excitedly. 'The Tales of Marty Martian' was his favourite bedtime story.

"Not now darling. It's time for bed. Goodnight," his mum replied as she tucked him in.

Ben snuggled into his blankets and soon found himself drifting off to sleep.

Suddenly Ben woke up! Why was he awake?
Then he heard it, a strange humming sort of noise. He listened carefully. It was coming from outside his bedroom window.

Quietly he hopped out of bed and put on his slippers (he didn't want to wake up Mum). Then he tiptoed over and opened the window just a crack.

"Zzwweeeee!!!" In through the window zoomed a... a... a... Ben didn't know what it was. It was hard to get a good look at it since it was zipping all around his bedroom.

From what he could see, it was shaped like a football. Not a proper pumped up one, it was more like one that had a hole in it.

"Cool!" said Ben and at once the thing stopped behaving like a crazy mosquito and began to hover over Ben's desk. A beam of light shone down and from it emerged the smallest alien Ben had ever seen. (Not that Ben had ever seen an alien before, but he was sure they were supposed to be bigger.)

"He looks pretty harmless," Ben said to himself.
But was he in for a surprise!

FEATURES: STRUCTURE LANGUAGE

STRUCTURE	LANGUAGE
Cliffhanger ending	Adverb
Complication	Direct speech
Orientation – characters and setting	Noun group
Resolution	Past tense
Series of events	Third person
	Time connective

Text sample: Narrative – Science fiction genre

Title: There's an Alien in my Bedroom!
Audience: Young children
Purpose: To entertain – bedtime story *Format: Picture book*

FEATURES

- Orientation – characters and setting
- Noun group
- Third person
- Series of events
- Time connective
- Adverb
- Complication
- Past tense
- Direct speech
- Simile
- Resolution
- Cliffhanger ending

There's an Alien in My Bedroom

"..... and so Flobot and Marty Martian lived happily ever after," finished Mum.

"Read it again!" Ben cried excitedly. 'The Tales of Marty Martian' was his favourite bedtime story.

"Not now darling. It's time for bed. Goodnight," his mum replied as she tucked him in.

Ben snuggled into his blankets and soon found himself drifting off to sleep.

Suddenly Ben woke up! Why was he awake? Then he heard it, a strange humming sort of noise. He listened carefully. It was coming from outside his bedroom window.

Quietly he hopped out of bed and put on his slippers (he didn't want to wake up Mum). Then he tiptoed over and opened the window just a crack.

"Zzwweeeee!!!" In through the window zoomed a... a... a... Ben didn't know what it was. It was hard to get a good look at it since it was zipping all around his bedroom.

From what he could see, it was shaped like a football. Not a proper pumped up one, it was more like one that had a hole in it.

"Cool!" said Ben and at once the thing stopped behaving like a crazy mosquito and began to hover over Ben's desk. A beam of light shone down and from it emerged the smallest alien Ben had ever seen. (Not that Ben had ever seen an alien before, but he was sure they were supposed to be bigger.)

"He looks pretty harmless," Ben said to himself. But was he in for a surprise!

IMAGINATIVE TEXTS | FAIRYTALES

Purpose: Fairytales are often seen as being stories just for young children. They are imaginary and have characters such as princes, witches and talking animals. They are usually set long ago in an **indistinct** time. They are written to entertain or amuse the reader. They are also useful tools for teaching young children about values and behaviour as many narratives have a **moral** or a message at the end.

STRUCTURE CORE FEATURES	ADVANCED FEATURES
orientation – sets the scene by creating setting time and place, and introducing characters. Characters are often magical or animals that can talk. Often 'Once upon a time…'	set an 'atmosphere' – give details about character description and personality
complication – there is a conflict or a problem that affects the setting or the characters. One character takes a 'hero' role.	a series of related or unrelated problems that reach a climax
resolution – the problem is solved	one or more of the problems may be unresolved or only partially resolved. The main character is changed by the experience.
ending – the normal pattern of life returns for the characters	make explicit how the character/s have been changed and what has been learnt (moral)

LANGUAGE CORE FEATURES	ADVANCED FEATURES
nouns to name characters	extended noun groups
adjectives to describe setting and characters	adverbial phrases to describe action
action verbs	saying and thinking verbs
past tense	written in first person
dialogue for direct speech	personification
time connectives and conjunctions	similes and metaphors for description
written in third person	

Key features: Traditional narrative – Fairytale genre

Read the example fairytale narrative below.
Can you find the key features of its structure and language? Use the features box to help you look.

The Three Little Wolves and Big Bad Pig

Once upon a time deep in the forest lived three little wolves with their mother.

Every day the wolves' mother would go out searching for food, while the little wolves played.

One day, however, the little wolves' mother did not return. They waited and they waited but still she did not come back.

The next morning there was a loud knock on the front door. The eldest wolf tried to peek under the door. "Wh…wh…who is it?" he enquired timidly.

"Why it is I, your friendly sales-pig. Can I come in?"

The little wolves knew that their mother had always warned them never to talk to strangers, so they called out, "No, not by the fur on our fluffy little tails. We will not let you in."

The Big Bad Pig was not impressed by their refusal. "If you don't let me in, I will slide down your chimney and use your tails to decorate my hat!"

What were the little wolves to do? They huddled together in the kitchen and worked out a cunning plan.

"If you want our tails to decorate your hat, you'll have to come and get them!" they called to the pig.

This made him very angry indeed. So the Big Bad Pig climbed up onto the roof and stuffed himself into the chimney. But he was too fat to fit and he got stuck.

Meanwhile, the three little wolves had built a raging fire under the chimney and spent the next couple of days feasting on smoked bacon for breakfast, lunch and dinner.

FEATURES: STRUCTURE LANGUAGE

Complication 1
Complication 2
Traditional orientation
Resolution

Action verbs
Adverbial phrase
Direct speech written in present tense
Noun groups
Saying verbs

Talking animals
Time connectives to sequence events
Written in past tense

Text sample: Narrative – Fairytale genre

Title: The Three Little Wolves and the Big Bad Pig
Audience: Young children
Purpose: To entertain – bedtime story *Format: Illustrated text*

FEATURES	The Three Little Wolves and Big Bad Pig
Traditional orientation	Once upon a time deep in the forest lived three little wolves with their mother.
Written in past tense	Every day the wolves' mother would go out searching for food, while the little wolves played.
Complication 1	One day, however, the little wolves' mother did not return. They waited and they waited but still she did not come back.
Time connectives to sequence events	The next morning there was a loud knock on the front door. The eldest wolf tried to peek under the door. "Wh...wh...who is it?" he enquired timidly.
Talking animals	"Why it is I, your friendly sales-pig. Can I come in?"
Direct speech written in present tense	The little wolves knew that their mother had always warned them never to talk to strangers, so they called out, "No, not by the fur on our fluffy little tails. We will not let you in."
Complication 2	The Big Bad Pig was not impressed by their refusal. "If you don't let me in, I will slide down your chimney and use your tails to decorate my hat!"
Adverbial phrase	What were the little wolves to do? They huddled together in the kitchen and worked out a cunning plan.
Noun groups	"If you want our tails to decorate your hat, you'll have to come and get them!" they called to the pig.
Saying verbs	This made him very angry indeed. So the Big Bad Pig climbed up onto the roof and stuffed himself into the chimney. But he was too fat to fit and he got stuck.
Action verbs	
Resolution	Meanwhile, the three little wolves had built a raging fire under the chimney and spent the next couple of days feasting on smoked bacon for breakfast, lunch and dinner.

IMAGINATIVE TEXTS POETRY

Poetry is very different to any other text type. In poetry, words are connected, not always in grammatically correct sentences, but they are linked by meaning and emotion.

Each genre within the text type of poetry has its own requirements for how it is organised and what structure it uses. Below are some common forms of poetry and their features.

The purpose of poetry is to capture the emotion of an object or event. Its rich use of language aims to intensify the reader's senses and imagination. Poetic language often has a natural rhyme or rhythm and is best understood when read aloud.

For more detail about poetic tools, please refer to the vocabulary section later in the *Writer's Guide*.

Key features: Poetry

Read the example poetry texts on the following pages.
Can you find the key features of their structure and language? Use the features boxes to help you look.

GENRE: ACROSTIC

Stars shine bright upon my bed
Tell me stories before I rest
Across the dark night sky you dance
Reaching out to heaven
Softly softly sleep

FEATURES: STRUCTURE

No title
Word written vertically down the page
Each line starts with the first letter of the topic word

Text samples: Poetry

Genre: ACROSTIC
Audience: Children before they go to bed
Purpose: To soothe and entertain
Format: Poster

FEATURES

No Title

Word written vertically down the page

Each line starts with the first letter of the topic word

Stars shine bright upon my bed
Tell me stories before I rest
Across the dark night sky you dance
Reaching out to heaven
Softly softly sleep

GENRE: FREE VERSE

Rain

Can you imagine, rain,
Falling from the sky,
Cold and wet upon your face,
Splashing to the ground,
Just imagine, rain.

FEATURES: STRUCTURE LANGUAGE

STRUCTURE
- Title
- A single stanza with 5 lines
- A circular pattern

LANGUAGE
- Lines in the middle to describe the topic

Genre: FREE VERSE
Audience: School students
Purpose: To entertain and evoke a personal response in the reader
Format: Picture book

FEATURES

Title — **Rain**

A single stanza with 5 lines

A circular pattern — Can you imagine, rain, / Just imagine, rain.

Lines in the middle to describe the topic — Cold and wet

Rain

Can you imagine, rain,
Falling from the sky,
Cold and wet upon your face,
Splashing to the ground,
Just imagine, rain.

GENRE: CINQUAIN

Food

Eat food
delicious food
cakes, pies, lollies and more
breakfast, lunch, don't forget dinner
I'm full!

FEATURES: STRUCTURE

Title of topic
5-line poem
Line 1 – 2 syllables
Line 2 – 4 syllables
Line 3 – 6 syllables
Line 4 – 8 syllables
Line 5 – 2 syllables – with a twist or a surprise comment

Genre: CINQUAIN
Audience: Students studying food
Purpose: To encourage group discussion of healthy and unhealthy food
Format: Poster for fun food

FEATURES

Title of topic — **Food**

5-line poem

Line 1 – 2 syllables — Eat food

Line 2 – 4 syllables — delicious food

Line 3 – 6 syllables — cakes, pies, lollies and more

Line 4 – 8 syllables — breakfast, lunch, don't forget dinner

Line 5 – 2 syllables – with a twist or a surprise comment. — I'm full!

GENRE: HAIKU

Wind

Gently tickles trees

Playful leaves as branches sway

Invisible thief

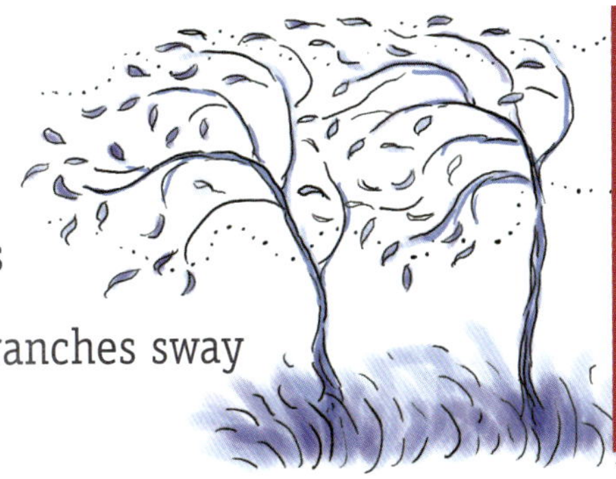

FEATURES: STRUCTURE

Title
3-line poem (Japanese form)
Used to describe nature

Line 1 – 5 syllables
Line 2 – 7 syllables
Line 3 – 5 syllables

Genre: HAIKU
Audience: Students studying spring weather
Purpose: To describe the wind using emotions
Format: Poster

FEATURES

Title — **Wind**

3-line poem
(Japanese form) Used to describe nature

Line 1 – 5 syllables — Gently tickles trees

Line 2 – 7 syllables — Playful leaves as branches sway

Line 3 – 5 syllables — Invisible thief

IMAGINATIVE TEXTS | DRAMATIC PLAY

Purpose: A play is a narrative that has been written for a dramatic performance. A play can enable the audience to take on another person's perspective as they explore difficult issues and complex relationships. Writers of plays do not have the same freedom that 'story' writers have in developing characters, as they have to establish the characters through what they say and do instead of using lots of description about them.

STRUCTURE CORE FEATURES	ADVANCED FEATURES
a title to introduce topic or setting of the play	
list of characters	briefly describe the characters
play is divided up into large sections called Acts. Each Act is briefly described.	each Act is divided into smaller sections called Scenes
character names are written in capitals to inform reader of when they are to be on stage and speaking	stage directions are written in italics to tell actors how to look and behave
orientation to introduce the setting and/or characters	
complication – there is a problem	in longer plays there are many scenes to set up multiple complications
resolution – the problem is solved	
use a new line when a different character speaks – no speech marks	

LANGUAGE CORE FEATURES	ADVANCED FEATURES
written in first and second person as the characters talk to each other	a character may appeal directly to the audience for assistance or understanding
lots of punctuation to show the actors how to use verbal expression	soliloquy – when a character talks by him/herself so that the audience can understand his/her thoughts and feelings

Key features: Dramatic play

Read the example dramatic play below.
Can you find the key features of its structure and language? Use the features box to help you look.

FEATURES:
STRUCTURE
LANGUAGE

Actors' names in capitals when they speak

Complication

Ending – audience understands meaning for character's feelings

List of characters

New line for a different character speaking

Orientation

Resolution

Scene is briefly described

Stage directions in italics. Actor does not say those words.

Title to set scene

Actors need to pay attention to the punctuation for expression

Two Fleas in a Boot

Characters: Neville *(a flea)*
Nigel *(a flea)*

ACT 1

SCENE 1 *(outside back door of an old house)*

NEVILLE: You awake Nigel?

NIGEL: *(yawning)* Yeah Nev … what's up?

NEVILLE: Uh nothing much. Just thinkin'.

NIGEL: Thinkin'? That must hurt. *(pause while Nigel scratches)* Whatcha thinkin' about?

NEVILLE: I was thinkin' that we need a new home.

NIGEL: What for? This one's good enough isn't it? I mean does it stink?

NEVILLE: *(pause)* Yeah.

NIGEL: Well … is it damp and musty?

NEVILLE: *(pause)* Yeah.

NIGEL: Do we get to bite stuff in it?

NEVILLE: *(pause)* Yeah.

NIGEL: Well then. What's not to love about home sweet home?

NEVILLE: It's just that, I miss Rover. *(sniffs)*

NIGEL: I know mate … I know. *(puts leg around Neville)*

Text sample: Dramatic play

Title: Two Fleas in a Boot
Audience: Live audience
Purpose: To entertain and amuse
Format: Reader's Theatre

FEATURES

Features	
Title to set scene	**Two Fleas in a Boot**
List of characters	Characters: Neville *(a flea)* Nigel *(a flea)*
	ACT 1
Scene is briefly described	SCENE 1 *(outside back door of an old house)*
Orientation	NEVILLE: You awake Nigel?
Actors' names in capitals when they speak	NIGEL: *(yawning)* Yeah Nev … what's up?
	NEVILLE: Uh nothing much. Just thinkin'.
Stage directions in italics. Actor does not say those words.	NIGEL: Thinkin'? That must hurt. *(pause while Nigel scratches)* Whatcha thinkin' about?
Complication	NEVILLE: I was thinkin' that we need a new home.
Actors need to pay attention to the punctuation for expression	NIGEL: What for? This one's good enough isn't it? I mean does it stink?
	NEVILLE: *(pause)* Yeah.
	NIGEL: Well … is it damp and musty?
New line for a different character speaking	NEVILLE: *(pause)* Yeah.
	NIGEL: Do we get to bite stuff in it?
	NEVILLE: *(pause)* Yeah.
Resolution	NIGEL: Well then. What's not to love about home sweet home?
Ending – audience understands meaning for character's feelings	NEVILLE: It's just that, I miss Rover. *(sniffs)*
	NIGEL: I know mate … I know. *(puts leg around Neville)*

IMAGINATIVE TEXTS ANECDOTE

Purpose: Anecdotes are written to relate an incident or event in a humorous or unusual way. They are similar to recounts because they retell an event, but they are imaginative in that they are funny and tend to stretch the truth just a little bit. They are an important part of our social lifestyle, as we get to know each other by sharing personal stories such as anecdotes.

Anecdotes can be written as a stand alone text, such as letters sent in to magazines for humorous columns like 'Mere Male' and 'Miss Five', or they can be part of a larger text, such as an anecdote told by a character in a narrative or novel.

STRUCTURE CORE FEATURES	ADVANCED FEATURES
single sentence to set the scene	
introduction to state when, where and who	
usually written in a single paragraph	written in multiple paragraphs to extend the detail
middle to tell of a problem and describe how the characters try to deal with the problem	
ending to solve the problem	final line is a punch line – the last part of a joke so the audience understands it
written from personal knowledge or experience	
dialogue (direct or reported speech) is used throughout the text	

LANGUAGE CORE FEATURES	ADVANCED FEATURES
often written in first person	
use reported speech	can use direct speech as a quote
use adverbs	
use conjunctions to sequence and explain causes of behaviour/events	
use thinking verbs	

Key features: Anecdote

Read the example anecdote below.
Can you find the key features of its structure and language? Use the features box to help you look.

Remember – brushing teeth is very important!

I remember my mother telling me and my sister this when we were kids, every night before we went to bed. But I never thought my three-year-old son would take it so seriously.

I was cleaning up in the kitchen one morning after breakfast when young Jayden came in complaining that the dog had eaten his toothbrush. When I asked him why the dog ate his toothbrush, he said that he had been trying to clean Max's teeth. I thought carefully about what to say before responding with, "Dogs don't need to clean their teeth like we do." I added that I would get him a new toothbrush because it would be yucky to use a toothbrush with dog slobber on it!

Thinking I had solved the problem, I got back to cleaning. But I was interrupted not two minutes later by Jayden handing me my toothbrush. I asked him why and almost fainted when he said that this one had to be thrown out because he had cleaned Max's teeth with it last week and it had doggy slobber on it too!

FEATURES: STRUCTURE LANGUAGE

STRUCTURE	LANGUAGE
Complication	Adverb
Heading of magazine article	Conjunction
How the characters react to the problem	Direct speech
Introduction: Who, Where, When	Reported speech
Punchline	
Resolution	
Set the scene	

Text sample: Anecdote

Purpose: To tell a funny short story
Audience: Other mums
Format: Article in magazine

FEATURES

Feature	Text
Heading of magazine article	**Remember – brushing teeth is very important!**
Set the scene	I remember my mother telling me and my sister this when we were kids, every night before we went to bed. But I never thought my three-year-old son would take it so seriously.
Introduction: Who, Where, When; Complication; Reported speech; Direct speech; How the characters react to the problem; Conjunction	I was cleaning up in the kitchen one morning after breakfast when young Jayden came in complaining that the dog had eaten his toothbrush. When I asked him why the dog ate his toothbrush, he said that he had been trying to clean Max's teeth. I thought carefully about what to say before responding with, "Dogs don't need to clean their teeth like we do." I added that I would get him a new toothbrush because it would be yucky to use a toothbrush with dog slobber on it!
Resolution; Adverb; Punchline	Thinking I had solved the problem, I got back to cleaning. But I was interrupted not two minutes later by Jayden handing me my toothbrush. I asked him why and almost fainted when he said that this one had to be thrown out because he had cleaned Max's teeth with it last week and it had doggy slobber on it too!

INFORMATIVE TEXTS | RECOUNT

Purpose: A recount tells what has happened. These past events are written about in chronological order, the time order in which they occurred. There are two broad categories of recount. One is a factual recount, which not only documents a series of events but also interprets and evaluates the experience in some way. The second is a literary recount, which is to retell a series of events for entertainment. Here the narrator or story teller has an emotional response to the events.

Recounts may take a variety of text forms such as historical diaries, detailed observations over time, police records, television interviews, eyewitness accounts and newspaper articles.

STRUCTURE

CORE FEATURES	ADVANCED FEATURES
orientation – gives details about who, when and where	covers complex issues
series of events – each event is usually written using a separate paragraph and following chronological order	order of events may be mixed if using techniques such as flashback and hindsight
a personal comment or an evaluation of the events and their implications	a reorientation to complete the writing and refer back to the beginning of the recount

LANGUAGE

CORE FEATURES	ADVANCED FEATURES
avoid use of 'then' – use varied conjunctions and connectives to link events	passive voice can be used at times so the writer can leave out the person doing the action
use of nouns and noun groups to describe people and things	
written in past tense	vary action verbs to build word chains and avoid repetition
use of adverbs and adverbial phrases to indicate time and place	use of technical vocabulary to make text more authentic and credible
write in 1st or 3rd person	
use evaluative language	structure sentences with important information at the beginning
use of reported speech not direct speech	
reference your work	

Key features: Factual recount

Read the example recount below.
Can you find the key features of its structure and language? Use the features box to help you look.

The history of human involvement in Mars has been relatively short. Only recently has mankind taken up the challenge to explore the planet Mars and try to find out if it has ever, or could ever, support life.

Ever since recorded history began, mankind has been fascinated by what lay beyond Earth. Yet it wasn't until 1971 that an orbiting spacecraft called Mariner 9 observed Mars and found that there were a number of canyons and channels that appeared to have been carved out of the rocky landscape by floods and rivers.

Several years later, in 1976, two Viking spacecraft landed on Mars and took samples of soil. Unfortunately for scientists at the time, when they were analysed, the samples showed no evidence of life either then or in the past.

But NASA did not end the quest with that disappointment. Two decades later, in 1995, they sent out the Mars Pathfinder. Upon landing, the Pathfinder sent out a small roving vehicle known as Sojourner, to continue the collection of information. However, Sojourner's mission was short lived due to technical difficulties.

At the turn of the century, in 2001, NASA sent out another mission known as the Mars Odyssey Orbiter. They followed this up in 2004 with two rovers, the Spirit and Opportunity, which found evidence that water had once existed on Mars.

Recently, in July 2008, the NASA spacecraft Phoenix landed on the polar region of Mars. Its mission was to dig up samples of the frozen soil and to heat it up to see if there was water trapped in the soil. And there was! Now scientists have concrete evidence that water can be found on Mars.

It was a crucial discovery that will be certain to lead to more missions to Mars in the future. (Perlman D. 2008, Hearst Communications Inc.)

FEATURES: STRUCTURE LANGUAGE

STRUCTURE	LANGUAGE
Event 1	Adverbial phrase
Event 2	Complex noun group
Event 3	Past tense
Events 4 & 5	Reference
Event 6	Time connectives
Evaluative comment	Written in third person
Orientation – who and where	

Text sample: Factual recount

Title: Exploration of Mars
Audience: Students with limited knowledge of the history of Mars exploration.
Purpose: To inform of significant events in our search for life on Mars
Format: Article in science magazine

FEATURES	
Orientation – who and where	The history of human involvement in Mars has been relatively short. Only recently has mankind taken up the challenge to explore the planet Mars and try to find out if it has ever, or could ever, support life.
Event 1 Complex noun group	Ever since recorded history began, mankind has been fascinated by what lay beyond Earth. Yet it wasn't until 1971 that an orbiting spacecraft called Mariner 9 observed Mars and found that there were a number of canyons and channels that appeared to have been carved out of the rocky landscape by floods and rivers.
Event 2 Time connectives	Several years later, in 1976, two Viking spacecraft landed on Mars and took samples of soil. Unfortunately for scientists at the time, when they were analysed, the samples showed no evidence of life either then or in the past.
Event 3 Adverbial phrase Events 4 & 5	But NASA did not end the quest with that disappointment. Two decades later, in 1995, they sent out the Mars Pathfinder. Upon landing, the Pathfinder sent out a small roving vehicle known as Sojourner, to continue the collection of information. However, Sojourner's mission was short lived due to technical difficulties.
Written in third person Event 6	At the turn of the century, in 2001, NASA sent out another mission known as the Mars Odyssey Orbiter. They followed this up in 2004 with two rovers, the Spirit and Opportunity, which found evidence that water had once existed on Mars.
Past tense Evaluative comment	Recently, in July 2008, the NASA spacecraft Phoenix landed on the polar region of Mars. Its mission was to dig up samples of the frozen soil and to heat it up to see if there was water trapped in the soil. And there was! Now scientists have concrete evidence that water can be found on Mars. It was a crucial discovery that will be certain to lead to more missions to Mars in the future.
Reference	(Perlman D. 2008, Hearst Communications Inc.)

INFORMATIVE TEXTS — REPORT

Purpose: Reports are also referred to as 'Information Reports' because they are used to organise and present factual information. They usually describe a class or group of things that may be natural (plants, countries, animals, volcanoes) or constructed (computers, transport, power stations). Information reports require a lot of research before you start writing.

Information reports appear in text books and reference books such as encyclopaedias. They cover areas such as natural science, technology, geology, geography and medical science. Scientific reports provide information about plants and animals. The organism is classified into a group according to set **criteria** and then various aspects of its appearance, diet and habitat are described.

Technological reports provide information about computers, space and engineering. They begin with a general statement of the topic and continue with paragraphs to describe different aspects of the type of machine, its appearance, its power, its functions and its history.

Sociological reports provide information about people, countries and cultures. They begin by giving a general statement about the topic and then providing details in separate paragraphs about language, government, history and trade.

STRUCTURE

CORE FEATURES	ADVANCED FEATURES
general statement or classification	visual items such as diagrams and charts
a series of paragraphs to describe different features of the topic	subheadings to organise information
a conclusion or rounding off statement	
use headings and subheadings	labelled diagrams / tables / charts

LANGUAGE

CORE FEATURES	ADVANCED FEATURES
general nouns not particular nouns	relating verbs to link features
formal language	use of passive voice
use short simple sentences	use of complex sentences
written in third person	limited use of personal pronouns
comparative adjectives	prepositional phrases
use of present tense	
time connectives	
longer noun groups for description	
technical vocabulary	
reference your work	

Key features: Sociological report – Geography World

Read the example information report below.
Can you find the key features of its structure and language? Use the features box to help you look.

Country:	EAST TIMOR
Location:	Oceania, Southeast Asia, 640 km northwest of Darwin, Australia
Climate:	tropical, hot and humid
Population:	approximately 950 000
Capital:	Dili
Language:	Tetum (a Malayo/Polynesian language) and Portuguese
Currency:	US dollar / centavo coins
Environment:	Mountainous, where floods and landslides are common. There is some irrigated land which is used for farming. The country is subject to tropical cyclones.
Trade:	Natural resources such as gold, petroleum and natural gas.
History:	East Timor was colonised by Portugal in the 16th Century and remained so until 1975 when it was invaded and occupied by Indonesia. In 1976 Indonesia declared East Timor a province. Backed by the United Nations, East Timor proclaimed self-determination in 1999 and Indonesia relinquished control. On 20 May 2002, East Timor became an independent nation.

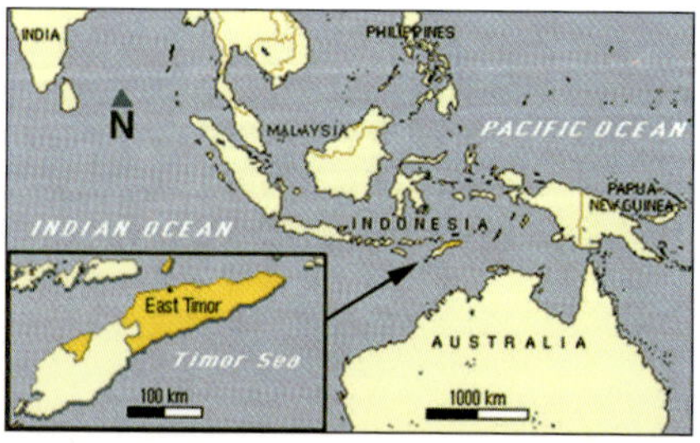

Map showing location of East Timor

(easttimorgovernment.com 2008)

FEATURES: STRUCTURE LANGUAGE

STRUCTURE	LANGUAGE
Conclusion	Noun groups
General statement of topic	Reference
Series of facts	Short simple sentences
Subheadings	Technical vocabulary
Visual elements	Third person

Text sample: Sociological Report – Geography World

Audience: Geography students *Purpose: To give facts about a topic*
Format: Page of an encyclopaedia

FEATURES

- General statement of topic
- Subheadings
- Series of facts
- Technical vocabulary
- Third person
- Noun groups
- Short simple sentences
- Conclusion
- Visual elements
- Reference

Country:	EAST TIMOR
Location:	Oceania, Southeast Asia, 640 km northwest of Darwin, Australia
Climate:	tropical, hot and humid
Population:	approximately 950 000
Capital:	Dili
Language:	Tetum (a Malayo/Polynesian language) and Portuguese
Currency:	US dollar / centavo coins
Environment:	Mountainous, where floods and landslides are common. There is some irrigated land which is used for farming. The country is subject to tropical cyclones.
Trade:	Natural resources such as gold, petroleum and natural gas.
History:	East Timor was colonised by Portugal in the 16th Century and remained so until 1975 when it was invaded and occupied by Indonesia. In 1976 Indonesia declared East Timor a province. Backed by the United Nations, East Timor proclaimed self-determination in 1999 and Indonesia relinquished control. On 20 May 2002, East Timor became an independent nation.

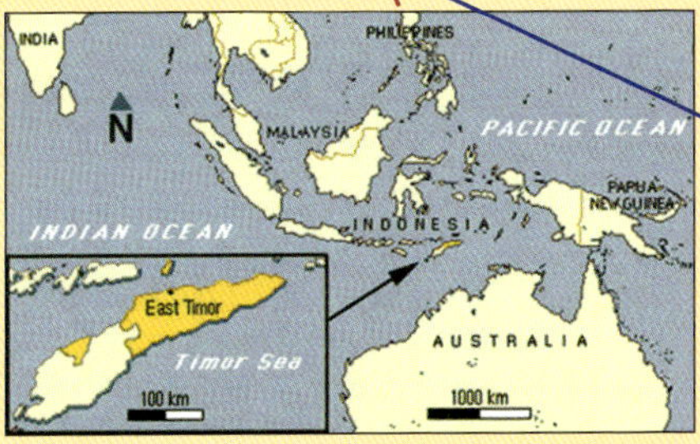

Map showing location of East Timor
(easttimorgovernment.com 2008)

INFORMATIVE TEXTS | EXPLANATION

Purpose: An explanation is written to explain how or why something in the world happens or how something works. They are written about actions rather than objects and are usually found in scientific or technical fields.

An explanation is a formal, professional text type that describes a process. It may be medical researchers explaining how a new medicine will work, or weather forecasters explaining why there will be a thunderstorm tomorrow, or a scientist explaining the life cycle of a butterfly.

STRUCTURE CORE FEATURES	ADVANCED FEATURES
title – often written in the form of a question to be answered – it gives a definition of the process	use words such as 'how…' or 'why…'
a general statement to introduce or identify the topic	extra information (facts) can be put into boxes
a series of events or logical steps in the process – written in separate paragraphs and showing cause and effect relationships	a concluding statement or paragraph
labelled diagrams / flow charts	

LANGUAGE CORE FEATURES	ADVANCED FEATURES
use of present tense	adverbial phrases to tell where and when actions occurred
general nouns and noun groups to build good descriptions	use of passive voice
non human subjects	
time conjunctions and connectives to link and sequence events	
use of technical language	
use of action verbs to explain the cause	
glossary for technical language	
reference your work	

Key features: Explanation – The Life Cycle of a Bee

Read the example information report below.
Can you find the key features of its structure and language? Use the features box to help you look.

How does a bee develop?

Bees are social insects that live in organised groups called colonies. Each colony lives in a hive and each hive has one queen, some drones or male bees, and lots and lots of worker bees. It is the drones' job to mate with the queen so that she can lay eggs.

A queen bee will begin laying eggs 10 days after mating. Each egg will be placed in a cell in the comb (inside the hive). She will lays about 3000 eggs a day for the rest of her life, about 2 years, and she will never leave the hive.

Four days after being laid, the eggs will hatch. At this stage they are called larvae. The larvae will be fed 'bee bread', which is a mixture of nectar and pollen.

On the ninth day after hatching, the larvae cells will be covered with wax as they begin the transformation into a pupa. During this stage, the pupa will not eat.

Finally, 21 days from the beginning of the life cycle, the pupa opens and an adult worker bee emerges, ready to begin life collecting pollen to make honey for the hive.

This life cycle for bees is known as **metamorphosis**. (kidcyber.com.au 2001)

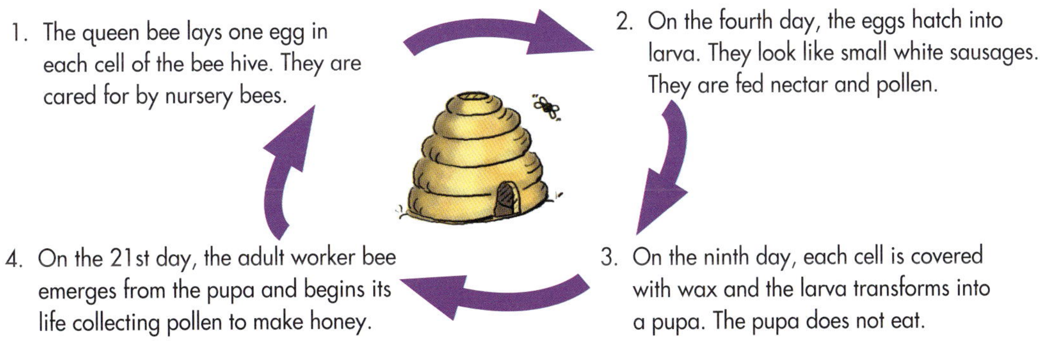

FEATURES: STRUCTURE LANGUAGE

STRUCTURE	LANGUAGE
Concluding statement	Action verbs
General statement to identify	Adverbial phrase
Labelled flow chart to support	Noun groups
New paragraph for each new event	Technical language
Series of steps in the process of bee life cycle	Time connectives
Title in the form of a question	Words in bold for glossary
	Reference

Text sample: Explanation – The Life Cycle of a Bee

Audience: Children researching
Purpose: To explain how a bee changes through its life
Format: Magazine feature

FEATURES

- **Title in the form of a question**
- **General statement to identify the topic**
- **Technical language**
- **Series of steps in the process of bee lifecycle**
- **New paragraph for each new event**
- **Action verbs**
- **Adverbial phrase**
- **Time connectives**
- **Noun groups**
- **Concluding statement**
- **Words in bold for glossary**
- **Reference**
- **Labelled flow chart to support explanation**

How does a bee develop?

Bees are social insects that live in organised groups called colonies. Each colony lives in a hive and each hive has one queen, some drones or male bees, and lots and lots of worker bees. It is the drones' job to mate with the queen so that she can lay eggs.

A queen bee will begin laying eggs 10 days after mating. Each egg will be placed in a cell in the comb (inside the hive). She will lay about 3000 eggs a day for the rest of her life, about 2 years, and she will never leave the hive.

Four days after being laid, the eggs will hatch. At this stage they are called larvae. The larvae will be fed 'bee bread', which is a mixture of nectar and pollen.

On the ninth day after hatching, the larvae cells will be covered with wax as they begin the transformation into a pupa. During this stage, the pupa will not eat.

Finally, 21 days from the beginning of the life cycle, the pupa opens and an adult worker bee emerges, ready to begin life collecting pollen to make honey for the hive.

This life cycle for bees is known as **metamorphosis**.

(kidcyber.com.au 2001)

1. The queen bee lays one egg in each cell of the bee hive. They are cared for by nursery bees.
2. On the fourth day, the eggs hat into larva. They look like small v sausages. They are fed nectar a pollen.
3. On the ninth day, each cell is cove with wax and the larva transforms a pupa. The pupa does not eat.
4. On the 21st day, the adult worker bee emerges from the pupa and begins its life collecting pollen to make honey.

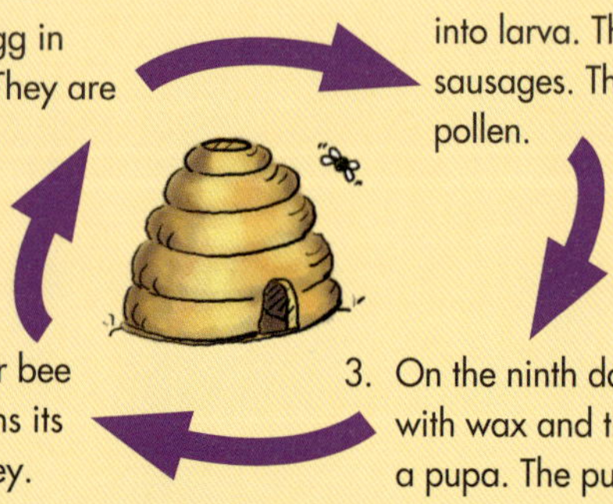

INFORMATIVE TEXTS | NEWS ARTICLE

Purpose: Newspaper articles are very similar to factual recounts. They are written to inform the reader of specific events. But news articles also want to appeal to the reader so they can sell as many newspapers, or get as many viewers as possible. As a result, many news articles use a layout that is eye-catching and a language style that is often emotional and dramatic.

It is important for the reader to understand that news articles are not always objective and that they may be biased towards one point of view, or deliberately provocative so that people talk about them.

STRUCTURE **CORE FEATURES**	**ADVANCED FEATURES**
headline – to attract the reader's attention	use reported speech to tell what other people said
by-line for name of reporter	
opening paragraph to tell the main information (what, where, who, when, why)	written in columns
a series of paragraphs to expand upon the events in order – give more details	larger articles use subheadings to group information
final paragraph to grab the attention of the reader	captions used for photos and illustrations

LANGUAGE **CORE FEATURES**	**ADVANCED FEATURES**
make it easy to read – lots of different people and ages will read it	use emotional language
use past tense	use provocative statements to make reader think about the topic
dramatic language choices	
time connectives to link events	
use of third person	

Key features: News article

Read the example news article below.
Can you find the key features of its organisation and language? Use the features box to help you look.

Storm Hits Local Suburb

by Win D. Hair

Willydilly emergency services volunteers were kept very busy last Friday night, after 95 km/hour winds battered the suburb.

Volunteers removed trees that blocked Ding Dong Street and Whos There Crescent, while local residents also pitched in by lending spare ladders and spotlights.

Emergency services received 59 calls for help after trees fell onto cars and caravans, and home awnings and fences collapsed.

The nearby suburb of Wingwang had a quieter period, with only a couple of calls regarding road signs that had fallen down and a billboard that was threatening to blow over.

Volunteers from Wingwang are travelling over to Willydilly to help with the storm clean-up.

So far no injuries have been reported.

There will be an information session for affected residents held tomorrow night in Wingwang Town Hall at 7:30 pm.

For details call: 00 9988 9988

FEATURES: STRUCTURE	LANGUAGE
Bold heading	Dramatic language
By-line for reporter's name	Past tense
Final paragraph to say what will happen next	Third person
Opening paragraph for most important information	Time connectives
Series of paragraphs detailing separate events	

Text sample: News article

Audience: People who live in Willydilly
Purpose: To inform residents of damage caused
Format: Newspaper article

FEATURES

Bold heading

By-line for reporter's name

Opening paragraph for most important information

Series of paragraphs detailing separate events

Past tense

Dramatic language

Third person

Time connectives

Final paragraph to say what will happen next

Storm Hits Local Suburb

by Win D. Hair

Willydilly emergency services volunteers were kept very busy last Friday night, after 95 km/hour winds battered the suburb.

Volunteers removed trees that blocked Ding Dong Street and Whos There Crescent, while local residents also pitched in by lending spare ladders and spotlights.

Emergency services received 59 calls for help after trees fell onto cars and caravans, and home awnings and fences collapsed.

The nearby suburb of Wingwang had a quieter period, with only a couple of calls regarding road signs that had fallen down and a billboard that was threatening to blow over.

Volunteers from Wingwang are travelling over to Willydilly to help with the storm clean-up.

So far no injuries have been reported.

There will be an information session for affected residents held tomorrow night in Wingwang Town Hall at 7:30 pm.

For details call: 00 9988 9988

INFORMATIVE TEXTS — PROCEDURE

Purpose: Procedures are written to instruct or direct the reader on how to do something by following a series of sequenced steps. They may take the form of a recipe, an instruction manual, sewing patterns, how to play a game, how to assemble a toy or travel directions.

The most important things to remember when writing procedures are:

- be accurate
- be concise (don't use too many words).

STRUCTURE

CORE FEATURES	ADVANCED FEATURES
a title that clearly identifies the purpose of the instructions	some may provide alternative steps in the sequence to achieve a slightly different result
subheadings for each section	some may provide warnings (in a box so they stand out)
an introductory statement that identifies the goal of the activity)	
a list of materials/ingredients or equipment needed	some may mention different consequences of the steps or the finished product
a series of numbered steps to be taken to achieve the goal – use numbered or bullet points	information at the end to enhance the finished project or to take it further
labelled diagrams or illustrations to show stages of progress or the finished product	

LANGUAGE

CORE FEATURES	ADVANCED FEATURES
make steps clear and to the point (don't use lots of descriptive words)	conditional language (if, but) used to show possible problems or warnings
use time connectives to sequence steps	
use adverbs and adjectives to clarify steps – tell when to do the step	give reasons to explain actions in each step
begin each step with an imperative verb	
use of technical language – use correct words so you don't confuse the reader	
use of present tense	

Key features: Procedure

Read the example procedural text below.
Can you find the key features of its structure and language? Use the features box to help you look.

FEATURES:
STRUCTURE
LANGUAGE

Information to enhance or extend the activity

Introduction to identify goal and gain reader's attention

List of ingredients

Numbered steps in the process

Subheadings

Title to show purpose of the instructions

Warning of possible consequence of inaction

Adverb

Imperative verbs

Present tense

Present tense

Technical language

Time connective (adverbial phrase)

How to Make an Omelette

In 'Cooking for Dummies' we hope to provide you with some simple kitchen skills so that you too can prepare a quick and healthy snack. Here we have come up with a delicious recipe for an omelette for one. If you have guests, simply double the ingredients.

Ingredients

3 eggs (large)	saucepan
ham	oil spray
cheese	spoon
1 tomato	fork
2 button mushrooms	

Method

1. Crack each egg into a bowl and mix thoroughly with a fork.
2. Slice the ham and grate the cheese before adding to the egg mix.
3. Finely chop the tomato and the mushrooms and add to the egg mix.
4. Gently stir the ingredients until combined.
5. Cover the base of the saucepan with oil spray, or the omelette will stick.
6. Preheat the saucepan to a moderate heat.
7. Pour the egg mixture into the saucepan and stir frequently so it doesn't burn.
8. When it is cooked, place omelette on a plate, or a piece of toast, and enjoy as a tasty snack.

For more adventurous cooks, try adding some fresh herbs or some onion for a different flavour.

Text sample: Procedure

Audience: Meal planners and people not confident with cooking
Purpose: To instruct reader on how to prepare food
Format: Recipe book

FEATURES

Title to show purpose of the instructions

Introduction to identify goal and gain reader's attention

Present tense

List of ingredients

Subheadings

Numbered steps in the process

Imperative verbs

Technical language

Adverb

Warning of possible consequence of inaction

Present tense

Time connective (adverbial phrase)

Information to enhance or extend the activity

How to Make an Omelette

In 'Cooking for Dummies' we hope to provide you with some simple kitchen skills so that you too can prepare a quick and healthy snack. Here we have come up with a delicious recipe for an omelette for one. If you have guests, simply double the ingredients.

Ingredients

3 eggs (large)	saucepan
ham	oil spray
cheese	spoon
1 tomato	fork
2 button mushrooms	

Method

1. Crack each egg into bowl and mix thoroughly with a fork.
2. Slice the ham and grate the cheese before adding to the egg mix.
3. Finely chop the tomato and the mushrooms and add to the egg mix.
4. Gently stir the ingredients until combined.
5. Cover the base of the saucepan with oil spray, or the omelette will stick.
6. Preheat the saucepan to a moderate heat.
7. Pour the egg mixture into the saucepan and stir frequently so it doesn't burn.
8. When it is cooked, place omelette on a plate, or a piece of toast, and enjoy as a tasty snack.

For more adventurous cooks, try adding some fresh herbs or some onion for a different flavour.

INFORMATIVE TEXTS BIOGRAPHY

Purpose: A biography is an account, or information and details, written about a person's life by someone else. You will find biographies written about famous people in encyclopaedias, nonfiction books that focus on a particular subject such as sport, history or politics, and of course on the internet.

Biographies are usually factual. But when they are written by someone close to the person, or acting on behalf of the person (with their permission), they may include opinions because they are written from a particular point of view.

STRUCTURE CORE FEATURES	ADVANCED FEATURES
introduction paragraph to give the reader a brief summary of the main idea	use a rhetorical opening
opening needs to gain interest of the reader	give personal opinions about the actions and influences of the person
events written in separate paragraphs to show chronological (time) order	
concluding paragraph to state the end of a career, to identify what the person will be most remembered for, or gives a fact about their lasting influence on others	end with a question to make the reader think deeply about the life and influences of the person

LANGUAGE CORE FEATURES	ADVANCED FEATURES
use third person	
use past tense	use present tense for some events or influences that are still happening
use passive voice to make it sound formal and factual	
use adverbial phrases to sequence and link events over time	
reference your work	

Key features: Biography – *Cathy Freeman*

Read the example biography below.
Can you find the key features of its structure and language? Use the features box to help you look.

http://www.cathyfreeman.com.au/

http://www.cathyfreeman.com.au/ | Cathy Freeman

Cathy Freeman was born in 1973 in the town of Mackay in Queensland. She became one of Australia's most famous athletes. As a youngster, Cathy was coached by her stepfather Bruce Barber and she won her first gold medal when she was 8 years old, at a school athletics carnival.

Due to her sporting abilities, Cathy won a scholarship to the Kooralbyn International School in Brisbane. So in 1989 her family also moved to Brisbane to be close to Cathy. At this time, she was no longer being coached by her stepfather, but by professional coach, Mike Danila.

In 1990, Cathy moved to Melbourne. That same year she participated in the Commonwealth Games in Auckland where she won a gold medal in the 4 ×100 m relay. This was the first gold medal awarded to an Aboriginal woman in an International athletics competition.

In the 1994 Commonwealth Games in Canada, she won both the 200 m and the 400 m events, following which she ran a lap of honour carrying both the Aboriginal and Australian flags. Such actions were very controversial.

However, controversy did not stop her and she went on to win the 400 m World Championship in 1997 and again in 1999.

But the highlight of her magnificent career occurred in the year 2000, when she lit the Olympic flame in Sydney and won her one and only Olympic Gold Medal in the 400 m.

Cathy Freeman retired from competitive athletics on 15 July 2003.

(Cathy Freeman, 2007 [online])

FEATURES: STRUCTURE LANGUAGE

Structure:
- Chronological order
- Comment on person's actions
- Concluding paragraph to state end of career
- Events in life written in separate paragraphs
- Graphic features of website format
- Introduction that gives brief summary of her importance
- Objective comment

Language:
- Adverbial phrase
- Factual information
- Past tense
- Reference
- Third person

Text sample: Biography – *Cathy Freeman*

Audience: Internet researchers
Purpose: To provide information about the life of Cathy Freeman
Format: Page of a website (webpage)

Cathy Freeman was born in 1973 in the town of Mackay in Queensland. She became one of Australia's most famous athletes. As a youngster, Cathy was coached by her stepfather Bruce Barber and she won her first gold medal when she was 8 years old, at a school athletics carnival.

Due to her sporting abilities, Cathy won a scholarship to the Kooralbyn International School in Brisbane. So in 1989 her family also moved to Brisbane to be close to Cathy. At this time, she was no longer being coached by her stepfather, but by professional coach, Mike Danila.

In 1990, Cathy moved to Melbourne. That same year she participated in the Commonwealth Games in Auckland where she won a gold medal in the 4 ×100 m relay. This was the first gold medal awarded to an Aboriginal woman in an International athletics competition.

In the 1994 Commonwealth Games in Canada, she won both the 200 m and the 400 m events, following which she ran a lap of honour carrying both the Aboriginal and Australian flags. Such actions were very controversial.

However, controversy did not stop her and she went on to win the 400 m World Championship in 1997 and again in 1999.

But the highlight of her magnificent career occurred in the year 2000, when she lit the Olympic flame in Sydney and won her one and only Olympic Gold Medal in the 400 m.

Cathy Freeman retired from competitive athletics on 15 July 2003.

(Cathy Freeman, 2007 [online])

Graphic features of website format

Introduction that gives brief summary of her importance

Past tense

Third person

Adverbial phrase

Events in life written in separate paragraphs

Chronological order

Factual information

Comment on person's actions

Objective comment

Concluding paragraph to state end of career

Reference

INFORMATIVE TEXTS DESCRIPTION

Purpose: A description is written to examine or describe features of a particular object, person or **phenomena**. Unlike an information report, which looks at a class or group of things, eg cats, roses, firefighters, a description looks at a specific subject.

Descriptions can be both factual and subjective. They can also involve the writer's imagination and emotions.

Descriptions are often found within a larger text, such as the description of the setting in a narrative or a character in a biography. Yet descriptions can also 'stand alone' as a separate piece of writing.

STRUCTURE

CORE FEATURES	ADVANCED FEATURES
an introduction about the topic	set the tone – factual or subjective
series of sentences to describe features of the topic	there may be some brief evaluation of the topic
rarely long enough for the use of paragraphs	
if a 'stand alone' description, it will have a conclusion which is a general statement about the topic	
if part of a longer text, it will have a conclusion that links the description to the other writing that follows	

LANGUAGE

CORE FEATURES	ADVANCED FEATURES
use of particular nouns, eg my toy	relating verbs
use of noun groups to add detail and visual imagery	thinking and feeling verbs
different adjectives (classify, numbering)	figurative language
action verbs to describe behaviour usually in present tense	
adverbs to detail time, place and behaviour	
similes and metaphors	

Key features: Description

Read the example description below.
Can you find the key features of its structure and language? Use the features box to help you look.

The Storm

I sit alone in my bedroom. I stare out the misty window and watch the heavy dark grey clouds roll across the sky. The sunlight is engulfed by a huge black glove. I feel trapped. Lightning starts to flicker in the blanketed sky – a torch flickering on, off, on, off. The rain starts to fall. Slowly at first, pitter patter pitter patter. Then heavier, as thousands of watery marbles drop from their bag onto my roof. I watch helplessly as the mighty wind picks leaves up off the ground and hurtles them into the sky like an invisible thief. The tree branches wave frantically for me to help them, but there is nothing I can do. The storm is too powerful.

FEATURES: STRUCTURE LANGUAGE

STRUCTURE	LANGUAGE
Conclusion – general statement of the topic	Action verbs
Introduction to set tone of topic	Metaphor
Separate sentences to describe different features	Noun group
Single paragraph	Personification
	Relating verbs
	Simile

Text sample: Description

Audience: Young children who have a shared experience of a storm
Purpose: To describe the features of a storm with imagery
Format: Stand alone text

FEATURES

Introduction to set tone of topic

Single paragraph

Relating verbs

Separate sentences to describe different features

Action verbs

Metaphor

Noun group

Simile

Personification

Conclusion – general statement of the topic

The Storm

I sit alone in my bedroom. I stare out the misty window and watch the heavy dark grey clouds roll across the sky. The sunlight is engulfed by a huge black glove. I feel trapped. Lightning starts to flicker in the blanketed sky – a torch flickering on, off, on, off. The rain starts to fall. Slowly at first, pitter patter pitter patter. Then heavier, as thousands of watery marbles drop from their bag onto my roof. I watch helplessly as the mighty wind picks leaves up off the ground and hurtles them into the sky like an invisible thief. The tree branches wave frantically for me to help them, but there is nothing I can do. The storm is too powerful.

PERSUASIVE TEXTS — EXPOSITION (ARGUMENT)

Purpose: An exposition is sometimes known as an argument. It is used to put forward one point of view, either for or against a particular idea. The writer's aim is to justify their point of view so that they will persuade the audience to agree with them.

Expositions can analyse, interpret or evaluate. They are often emotive and can sometimes be personal. They don't give a rounded view of the topic, but are selective in what they say and how their ideas are presented.

Expositions can be found in newspaper editorials, political campaign speeches, legal presentations in court and current affairs broadcasts.

STRUCTURE

CORE FEATURES	ADVANCED FEATURES
introductory statement that identifies the position of the writer – for or against the topic idea clearly	writers may choose to order arguments from strongest to weakest to make key points early
a series of arguments presented in separate paragraphs	arguments may be ordered from weakest to strongest to end on a high point
each argument needs ideas or examples to support it	each paragraph has one main idea to be elaborated on
writers need to think about their target audience and what arguments will catch their attention	
conclusion to restate the position and sum up and emphasise the main points	

LANGUAGE

CORE FEATURES	ADVANCED FEATURES
use general nouns, eg traffic, noise	use passive voice
use abstract nouns, eg bravery, policy	do not use personal pronouns
emotive words, eg destroy, brutal	use reported speech
use technical words to give ideas authority	
usually written in present tense	
use thinking verbs, eg believe, hope	
connectives, eg therefore, so, because	
adverbs, eg certainly, must	

Key features: Exposition – Protect Your Children's Future

Read the example exposition text below.
Can you find the key features of its structure and language? Use the features box to help you look.

Recently there has been much publicity over a system called 'Carbon Trading', with many people in the local community upset over how much it is going to cost. How can people be so narrow-minded? Yes, any system to save our environment is going to cost. Nothing in life is free. But what is the cost of inaction?

Our climate is warming up. That is an undisputed fact. What is the cost of inaction? Farmers will have to battle longer and harsher droughts. Food will become scarce and the poorer nations will be unable to afford to feed their people.

Furthermore, our weather patterns are becoming more unpredictable. What is the cost of inaction? Our cities and towns will be battered by more frequent fierce storms. Millions of dollars will be spent on clean-up programs and the rebuilding of damaged infrastructure.

As a result of climate change, every year we are losing our treasured and unique native wildlife. What is the cost of inaction? Since European settlement, over 200 species of mammals have become extinct and many more birds, reptiles and amphibians are on the endangered list. If we do not act, our children may never see a koala or a wombat in the wild.

If we, as a community, do not act now, no amount of money will be able to repair the damage in the future. The future benefits truly outweigh the present costs.

FEATURES: STRUCTURE LANGUAGE

STRUCTURE	LANGUAGE
Conclusion to restate position and sum up arguments	Connectives
Elaboration	Emotive language
Introduction to set the topic and state point of view	General noun
Main point	Present tense
Paragraphs to make separate arguments	Technical language

Text sample: Exposition – Protect Your Children's Future

Audience: Young adults
Purpose: To convince the reader to behave in a more environmentally friendly way
Format: Editorial

FEATURES

- **Introduction to set the topic and state point of view**
- **Emotive language**
- **Present tense**
- **Paragraphs to make separate arguments**
- **General noun**
- **Main point**
- **Elaboration**
- **Connectives**
- **Technical language**
- **Conclusion to restate position and sum up arguments**

Recently there has been much publicity over a system called 'Carbon Trading', with many people in the local community upset over how much it is going to cost. How can people be so narrow-minded? Yes, any system to save our environment is going to cost. Nothing in life is free. But what is the cost of inaction?

Our climate is warming up. That is an undisputed fact. What is the cost of inaction? Farmers will have to battle longer and harsher droughts. Food will become scarce and the poorer nations will be unable to afford to feed their people.

Furthermore, our weather patterns are becoming more unpredictable. What is the cost of inaction? Our cities and towns will be battered by more frequent fierce storms. Millions of dollars will be spent on clean-up programs and the rebuilding of damaged infrastructure.

As a result of climate change, every year we are losing our treasured and unique native wildlife. What is the cost of inaction? Since European settlement, over 200 species of mammals have become extinct and many more birds, reptiles and amphibians are on the endangered list. If we do not act, our children may never see a koala or a wombat in the wild.

If we, as a community, do not act now, no amount of money will be able to repair the damage in the future. The future benefits truly outweigh the present costs.

PERSUASIVE TEXTS | LETTERS TO THE EDITOR

Purpose: Letters to the editor are very similar to exposition or argument texts. They are written to try to convince others to agree with the views of the writer. Unlike expositions, which tend to deal with broad topics such as climate change or saving endangered animals, letters to the editor tend to deal with more specific topics. Since many newspapers are locally based, the issues tend to be ones of local or regional significance, not worldwide importance. Such letters are quite formal in nature.

STRUCTURE CORE FEATURES	ADVANCED FEATURES
writer's address at top left-hand corner	
date underneath writer's address	
address of recipient underneath date	
title or name of recipient	
introductory paragraph to state reason for writing	
series of paragraphs to state arguments for writers point of view with reasons and supporting evidence	towards the end may summarise main points
final paragraph to state action the writer wants taken	
formal sign off – 'Yours faithfully'	

LANGUAGE CORE FEATURES	ADVANCED FEATURES
written in present tense	use of rhetorical questions
written in first person	disguise opinion as fact
use of emotive language	
use of subjective language	
action and thinking verbs	
connectives to link ideas between paragraphs	

Key features: Letter to the Editor

Read the example letter to the editor below.
Can you find the key features of its structure and language? Use the features box to help you look.

Mr Crang Key
1 A Mupset Street
Dunbeena 1010

14th February 2009

The editor
Dunbeena Gazette

Dear Sir,

As a long-term resident of Dunbeena, I am frustrated, alarmed and even frightened by the inability of the government to provide us with a consistent ambulance emergency service. I have been forced to realise that local councillors and public servants are unable to understand the plight of our little community.

For the past six long months, Dunbeena residents have been without 24-hour ambulance coverage. Instead we have had to rely on the goodwill of the handful of community members with medical training to assist the sick and elderly.

Ambulance management and the government have sat on their hands, refusing to act to support the people who elect and pay them.

What we need are strong leaders who are willing to make decisions to benefit all members of the local community. We need them to fund the ongoing rostering of ambulance officers at Dunbeena station, and to commit to the building of a new and permanent ambulance station in the area.

Access to adequate emergency services is a right for all residents. You don't have to be Einstein to work out what should be done!

Yours faithfully,
Mr Crang Key
Dunbeena resident

FEATURES: STRUCTURE LANGUAGE

Conclusion to state action wanted
Date
Formal sign off
Introduction to state reason for writing

Name of recipient is unknown so use general title
Series of paragraphs to give arguments
Supporting evidence
Writer's name and address

Action verbs
Emotive language
Opinion disguised as fact
Subjective language
Written in first person

Text sample: Letter to the Editor

Audience: Local residents and government officials
Purpose: To persuade people to agree with writer's point of view
Format: Newspaper letter

FEATURES

Features	Letter
Writer's name and address	Mr Crang Key 1 A Mupset Street Dunbeena 1010
Date	14th February 2009
Recipient	The editor Dunbeena Gazette
Name of recipient is unknown so use general title	Dear Sir,
Introduction to state reason for writing **Emotive language**	As a long-term resident of Dunbeena, I am frustrated, alarmed and even frightened by the inability of the government to provide us with a consistent ambulance emergency service. I have been forced to realise that local councillors and public servants are unable to understand the plight of our little community.
Series of paragraphs to give arguments **Supporting evidence**	For the past six long months, Dunbeena residents have been without 24-hour ambulance coverage. Instead we have had to rely on the goodwill of the handful of community members with medical training to assist the sick and elderly.
Opinion disguised as fact	Ambulance management and the government have sat on their hands, refusing to act to support the people who elect and pay them.
Subjective language **Written in first person** **Action verbs**	What we need are strong leaders who are willing to make decisions to benefit all members of the local community. We need them to fund the ongoing rostering of ambulance officers at Dunbeena station, and to commit to the building of a new and permanent ambulance station in the area.
Conclusion to state action wanted	Access to adequate emergency services is a right for all residents. You don't have to be Einstein to work out what should be done!
Formal sign off	Yours faithfully, Mr Crang Key Dunbeena resident

PERSUASIVE TEXTS — ADVERTISMENT

Purpose: Advertising is a type of exposition. It promotes goods, services and activities such as encouraging people to donate money or attend special events. The aim is to persuade people to buy the product, or use the service. Advertisements use positive images and are directed at a specific target audience. They are often visually appealing and use catchy slogans.

Although the format of advertisements determines their overall layout, they all follow the same general structure.

Good or effective advertisements should have a strong purpose, a specific audience and be direct and to the point.

STRUCTURE CORE FEATURES	ADVANCED FEATURES
large headline to summarise the message	
headline needs to be bold, catchy and use powerful language	
copy – this is the writing of the advertisement. It can be set out in columns or boxes, but paragraphs are kept short and use simple language.	text boxes – set out in boxes and contain facts and statistics
illustrations – photos, cartoons, diagrams, graphs or charts to catch the reader's attention	layout to attract attention by using different fonts, font size and colour

LANGUAGE CORE FEATURES	ADVANCED FEATURES
use emotive language so the reader can identify with the need for the product or service	use stereotypes because they are easily recognised by the audience
use of strong adjectives	offer incentives
use a catchy slogan	
use superlatives, eg best	
talk directly to the audience, eg you will...	

Key features: Advertisement

Read the example advertisement below.
Can you find the key features of its structure and language? Use the features box to help you look.

FEATURES:
STRUCTURE
LANGUAGE

Bold heading to catch attention

Copy

Illustration to demonstrate a point

Appeal directly to the audience

Common stereotype

Incentives offered to encourage business

Personal pronoun

Powerful adjectives

Rhetorical questions to gain audience interest

Superlative

LITTLE BORING DAY SPA

Tired?? Worn out??
Hate early mornings??

Don't let Monday morning drag you down.

We believe that life as a student is way too stressful and that you and your friends deserve a break.

Why not leave the books, the tests, and the maths groups behind you and come and sample Little Boring's most relaxing day spa.

Upon arrival you will receive:

- a scalp massage
- light refreshments
- internationally renowned music therapy

SHOP 1 NOSTRESS STREET, LITTLE BORING
PHONE: 5317707

Text sample: Advertisement

Audience: Tired school students
Purpose: To persuade the reader to go to the spa
Format: Letter box brochure

FEATURES

Bold heading to catch attention

Rhetorical questions to gain audience interest

Common stereotype

Personal pronoun

Appeal directly to the audience

Illustration to demonstrate a point

Copy

Superlative

Powerful adjectives

Incentives offered to encourage business

LITTLE BORING DAY SPA

Tired?? Worn out??
Hate early mornings??

Don't let Monday morning drag you down.

We believe that life as a student is way too stressful and that you and your friends deserve a break.

Why not leave the books, the tests, and the maths groups behind you and come and sample Little Boring's most relaxing day spa.

Upon arrival you will receive:

- a scalp massage
- light refreshments
- internationally renowned music therapy

Group discounts available, so bring your friends!

SHOP 1 NOSTRESS STREET, LITTLE BORING
PHONE: 5317707

PERSUASIVE TEXTS — REVIEW

Purpose: A review is written to summarise and analyse a written text, or sometimes a movie or play. Some people think that a review and a response are the same thing, but they have some important differences. A review is more formal. Like a response, it gives the audience background information, but it also gives a summary of the content with fuller descriptions of characters and plot, and reflects on how these work together.

STRUCTURE CORE FEATURES	ADVANCED FEATURES
author's name	
title of text reviewed	
name of publisher and date published	
ISBN number – found on back cover	
opening sentence to set the context for the review and some background information	
text description – usually one paragraph to describe main characters or plot or content	use a series of paragraphs each one to describe a different aspect of the text
judgment – the writer evaluates the text and gives an overall opinion and a recommendation	use visual aids to enhance message

LANGUAGE CORE FEATURES	ADVANCED FEATURES
written in present tense	use past tense if the text uses an historical setting
thinking verbs	
persuasive language used for evaluation	connectives to sequence ideas when important events in text are summarised
noun groups	

Key features: Review – *Blake's Writer's Guide*

Read the example review text below.
Can you find the key features of its structure and language? Use the features box to help you look.

WHITFIELD, Merryn
Blake's Writer's Guide
Pascal Press, 2009
ISBN 978 1 921367 752 6

Written by an inspirational classroom teacher with over 15 years' experience, *Blake's Writer's Guide* is an essential tool for students looking to enhance their written expression. The book features a clear and easy-to-follow format and an extensive index means that you will always be able to find what you are looking for. Colour-coded text scaffolds aid the visual effectiveness of the text. Every tool or resource a writer would ever need to use is examined and explained in this comprehensive guide. From text type requirements to process writing, and from graphic organisers to tips for quality publishing, you will find it all here in easy-to-understand language. *Blake's Writer's Guide* is a must for every school and every student.

USER LEVEL: middle to upper primary
KLA: English
Price: $11.95

A Survey of Students from Blairmont Community School
"What do you think of the *Writer's Guide*?"

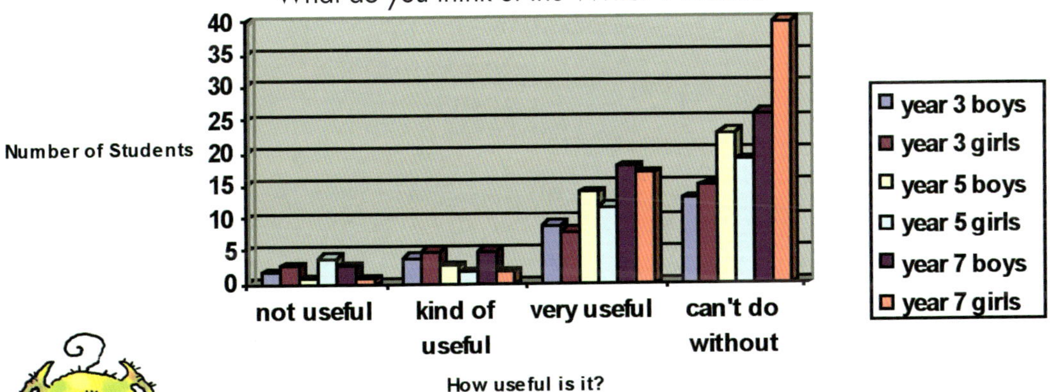

FEATURES: STRUCTURE LANGUAGE

Structure	Structure	Language
Evaluation	Publisher and date	Appeals directly to the reader
ISBN number	Recommendation	Noun groups
Name of text author	Text description	Persuasive language
Opening to give background information	Title of text	Present tense

Text sample: Review – *Blake's Writer's Guide*

Audience: Teachers who want to help students improve their writing
Purpose: To persuade the reader to buy the book
Format: Small article on a teacher resource website

FEATURES

- Name of text author
- Title of text
- Publisher and date
- ISBN number
- Opening to give background information
- Persuasive language
- Present tense
- Text description
- Noun groups
- Appeals directly to the reader
- Evaluation
- Recommendation

WHITFIELD, Merryn
Blake's Writer's Guide
Pascal Press, 2009
ISBN 978 1 921367 751 9

Written by an inspirational classroom teacher with over 15 years' experience, *Blake's Writer's Guide* is an essential tool for students looking to enhance their written expression. The book features a clear and easy-to-follow format and an extensive index means that you will always be able to find what you are looking for. Colour-coded text scaffolds aid the visual effectiveness of the text. Every tool or resource a writer would ever need to use is examined and explained in this comprehensive guide. From text type requirements to process writing, and from graphic organisers to tips for quality publishing, you will find it all here in easy-to-understand language. *Blake's Writer's Guide* is a must for every school and every student.

USER LEVEL: middle to upper primary
KLA: English
Price: $11.95

A Survey of Students from Blairmont Community School
"What do you think of the *Writer's Guide*?"

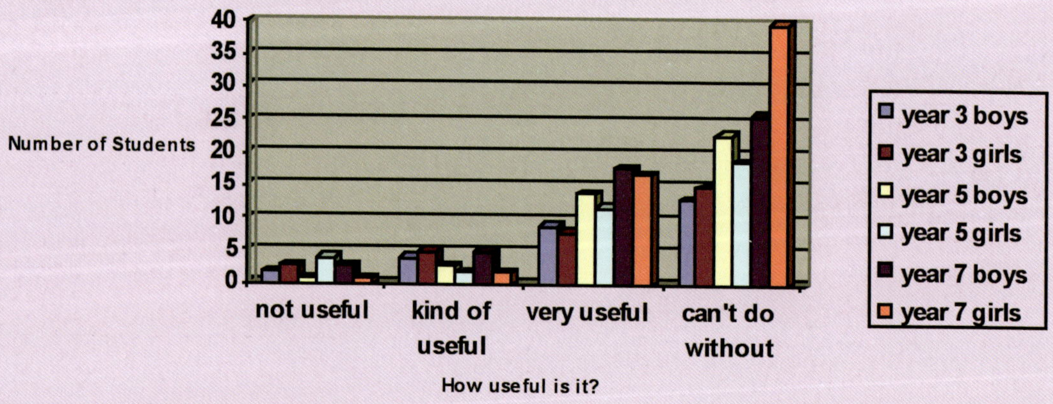

PERSUASIVE TEXTS — DISCUSSION

Purpose: A discussion looks at different points of view or opinions on a particular issue. It allows the reader to think about different perspectives before making an informed decision.

Discussion texts evaluate, analyse and interpret ideas and issues. They can be informal such as friendly conversations or talk back radio interviews. They can also be formal, such as political debates, newspaper articles or judgments in court.

STRUCTURE CORE FEATURES	ADVANCED FEATURES
a title to identify the topic or issue	
an introduction to state the position and provide background information	
a series of paragraphs giving arguments and supporting evidence in favour of the topic	a series of paragraphs giving arguments and supporting evidence – alternating: for, against, for, against
a series of paragraphs giving arguments and supporting evidence against the topic	
a conclusion to sum up the main points or give a recommendation	

LANGUAGE CORE FEATURES	ADVANCED FEATURES
use of present tense	adverbs to show manner, eg hopefully
use of general nouns for categories, eg homework	use of speech – both quoted and reported
use of noun groups to give concise information	
use of thinking and saying verbs	use of passive voice
use of comparative or contrasting adjectives	vary use of modality, eg must, should, perhaps
use of connectives to link arguments	
use of evaluative language	

Key features: Discussion – Should children have to do homework?

Read the example discussion text below.
Can you find the key features of its structure and language? Use the features box to help you look.

FEATURES:
STRUCTURE
LANGUAGE

A conclusion to sum up and make a recommendation

Alternating arguments for and against the topic

An opening statement that sets out the issue

Supporting evidence for arguments

Adverb of manner

Comparative adjective

Connectives

Emotive language

Evaluative language

Noun group

Present tense

Thinking verb

Mrs Wood: Homework this term will be given out on Monday mornings and you will need to hand it in on Friday before sport. Are there any questions?

Nikolas: Yeah. Why do we have to do homework in the first place? I reckon it's a waste of time.

Mrs Wood: I'm sorry you think that Nikolas because homework is an important part of your education. For a start, it helps you establish good work habits and time management skills. That way you learn how to organise your time so everything gets done when it needs to be done.

Nikolas: That doesn't help me. I have to spend so much time doing my homework that by the time I am finished it is dark and Mum won't let me go and play outside with my friends. Homework is ruining my social life.

Mrs Wood: Well, without doing your homework regularly, you are going to miss out on understanding the work we do in class. By practising activities like maths and reading at home, it will consolidate those ideas in your mind and you will find it easier to remember the details later.

Nikolas: I remember that homework is the most BORING thing and I hate it when my mum keeps looking over my shoulder asking questions about it. All I want to do is get it done as quickly as I can so I can check out my latest game.

Mrs Wood: I think it's great that your mum takes an interest in your homework. Homework is another way that the school can communicate with your parents to inform them about what is going on at school. It shows that they care about you and your education.

Nikolas: I guess so. But if I *have* to do homework, maybe there can be less of it!

Text sample: Discussion – Should children have to do homework?

Audience: Class 3/4 WG
Purpose: To present both sides of an issue
Format: Transcript of a spoken discussion for a drama performance

FEATURES

An opening statement that sets out the issue

Present tense

Thinking verb

Alternating arguments for and against the topic

Connectives

Noun group

Emotive language

Adverb of manner

Supporting evidence for arguments

Comparative adjective

Evaluative language

A conclusion to sum up and make a recommendation

Mrs Wood: Homework this term will be given out on Monday mornings and you will need to hand it in on Friday before sport. Are there any questions?

Nikolas: Yeah. Why do we have to do homework in the first place? I reckon it's a waste of time.

Mrs Wood: I'm sorry you think that Nikolas because homework is an important part of your education. For a start, it helps you establish good work habits and time management skills. That way you learn how to organise your time so everything gets done when it needs to be done.

Nikolas: That doesn't help me. I have to spend so much time doing my homework that by the time I am finished it is dark and Mum won't let me go and play outside with my friends. Homework is ruining my social life.

Mrs Wood: Well, without doing your homework regularly, you are going to miss out on understanding the work we do in class. By practising activities like maths and reading at home, it will consolidate those ideas in your mind and you will find it easier to remember the details later.

Nikolas: I remember that homework is the most BORING thing and I hate it when my mum keeps looking over my shoulder asking questions about it. All I want to do is get it done as quickly as I can so I can check out my latest game.

Mrs Wood: I think it's great that your mum takes an interest in your homework. Homework is another way that the school can communicate with your parents to inform them about what is going on at school. It shows that they care about you and your education.

Nikolas: I guess so. But if I *have* to do homework, maybe there can be less of it!

BIBLIOGRAPHY

Books

Classworks Literacy, Blake Education, Clayton South, 2004
Collins English Dictionary, Collins Publishing, Great Britain, 1986
Martin, Rodney, *Young Writer's Guide 4th Ed*, ERA Publications, 2007
Non Fiction Writing Scaffolds (series), Blake Education, Clayton South, 2008

Roget, Peter, *Roget's Thesaurus*, Great Britain, 1972
Story Writing Scaffolds (series), Blake Education, Clayton South, 2007
Targeting Text Middle Primary (series), Blake Education, Clayton South, 1999

Targeting Text Upper Primary (series), Blake Education, Clayton South, 1999

Writer's Notebook, Teacher Created Materials, Huntington Beach, 2006

Websites

Ager, Simon, 2008, www.omniglot.com/writing/definition.htm
East Timor Government, 2008, www.easttimorgovernment.com/index.htm
Kidcyber (Cathy Freeman), 2007, www.kidcyber.com.au/topics/Freemancathy.htm
Perlman, David, Hearst Communications Inc., 2008, www.sfgate.com/cgi-bin/article.cgi?f=/c/a/2008/07/16/MNOM11Q5E7.DTL
The Learning Centre, University of NSW, 2008, www.lc.unsw.edu.au/onlib/ref1.html
University of Bristol, 2008, www.bristol.ac.uk/visualidentity/house-style.html
University of North Carolina Writing Centre, 2008, www.unc.edu/depts/
Kidcyber (Bees), 2001, www.kidcyber.com.au

To reference other media types:

* A blog – (author name, year of blog posting, name of blog, URL address)
* CD-ROM – (title, year of recording, format, publisher, place of publication)
* Film/Video/TV – (title, year of recording, format, publisher, place of publication)
* Brochure – (author name, date published, name of article)
* Newspaper/Magazine – (title of article, newspaper name, date published, page)

(University of NSW, 2008)

GLOSSARY

abbreviation	A shortened form of a word eg – For example, St – street, Dr – doctor
accuracy	How correct or truthful something is
active voice	The subject of the sentence does the action
adjective	A word that describes a noun eg beautiful, soft, bumpy
adjectival phrase	A group of words that describe: how many, what kind, or who owns the 'thing'
adverb	A word that describes a verb eg quickly, loudly
adverbial phrase	A word or group of words that tells how, when or why an action is taking place
advertisement	A text used to persuade the audience to buy a product or service
anecdote	A short, funny story that is retold
annotated	Containing short notes of explanation
apostrophe	A punctuation mark to indicate missing letters in words or possession of an object
appropriate	Something that is proper or correct
argument	A text that shows only one point of view
arrogant	Acting self-important or more important than other people
audience	People who read a piece of writing
author	Person who writes poems, stories, plays or other texts
autobiography	A story written by you about your own life
bias	An unfair liking or disliking of something
bibliography	A list of books used to find information for a piece of writing
biography	The story of someone else's life
casual	Writing that is relaxed and informal
character	A person or a creature from a text
chronologically	Events that are sequenced in order of time
clause	A group of words with a verb that puts across an idea
coda	An addition to the end of a text, like an afterthought
colloquial	Words that are informal, slang or conversational
comma	A punctuation mark used to indicate separate clauses or items in a list (,)
command	An order or direction given to do something
communicate	To swap or give information through speech or writing
comparative	Word used to compare two or more objects eg bigger, thinner, happier
complication	Event in a text where something goes wrong
conclusion	The ending of a text
conjunction	A word used to join or link different parts of the same sentence eg and, so, but

context	The background or situation in which a piece of writing is set
credibility	Ideas or information which is reliable or trustworthy
cursive	Form of handwriting where letters join together (running writing)
description	Writing that describes the features of a place, person or object
dialogue	The writing down of speech between one or more characters
dictionary	Book which lists words and their meaning
directions	Instructions on how to do something or go somewhere
direct speech	Words actually spoken by a character eg "Stop!" said Mum
discussion	Piece of writing that examines two different points of view on a topic
draft	Rough, unfinished piece of work
drama	A play
edit	To revise a piece of writing looking at spelling and punctuation
editor	Person who edits writing
encyclopaedia	Book or series of books providing information on a variety of topics
epiphany	A moment when a character realises something important
evaluation	To make a judgment about an idea or a piece of writing
exclamation	A word or group of words that shows strong emotions
explanation	A piece of writing that explains how or why
exposition	A piece of writing that argues only one point of view on a particular topic
fact	A true statement that can be proven
fairytale	An imaginative narrative based in fantasy
fiction	Writing that is not based on fact – it is imaginative
figurative language	The creative way writers use the sound and meaning of words to describe
first person	Writing that uses personal pronouns such as I, me
flippant	Not being serious
fluency	The flow of words and sentences
font	A style of writing
footnote	Extra information about part of a text at the bottom of the page
formal language	Writing that uses words to sound important
format	How a piece of writing is set out on a page or in print
future tense	The verbs used express future actions eg I will go tomorrow.
genre	A category of writing based on style
glossary	A list of technical words and their meaning used in a text
grammar	The rules we use to make sense with words and sentences
graphic	Representing information using pictures
humour	Something funny
illustrator	Person who creates pictures for a text
imagery	The creative way writers use words to describe something
imaginary texts	Writing that is written from the imagination – pretend, not real
imperative	A command, a statement of something important

indecisive	Unable to make a decision
indirect speech	Reported speech – words not directly spoken eg He told me to stop.
informal	Not formal, relaxed and everyday language eg G'day
introduction	Beginning of a text to set the scene or introduce the topic
irony	Words that say one thing but mean something different
italic	Style of writing that slants to the right
literal	Language that is true or exact in its meaning
metamorphosis	A change of physical form
metaphor	Comparing two items by saying one is the other
moral	A lesson in appropriate behaviour
narrative	A story with a complication
narrator	Person who tells the events of the story in the text
noun	Name of a person, place or thing eg dog, house, brick
object	Something that is acted on by the subject of a sentence
onomatopoeia	Words that sound like the actions they represent eg bang, splash
opinion	A belief, not a fact
organisation	How the piece of writing is set out
orientation	The introduction to a piece of writing to set the scene and the characters
paragraph	Section of a text written about a particular event, idea or time
passive voice	The subject of the sentence is not doing the action
past tense	Where events being written about have already happened eg I ate my lunch.
personification	Non human objects or characters are given human traits or features
persuasion	Text used to change or influence another person's point of view
phenomena	Something that can be seen or experienced
phrase	A meaningful group of words in a sentence that does not contain a verb
plagiarism	Stealing someone else's work or ideas
play	A text to be performed by actors
preposition	A word that gives the position of an object eg under, above
present tense	Text where the verbs tell of events that are happening now eg I am happy.
procedure	Text written to give instructions
pronoun	Word used to replace a noun eg you, she
proofread	Rereading or checking writing for errors
provocative	To be deliberately annoying or upsetting
publish	To present a text for an audience
publisher	Person who publishes texts
punctuation	Marks made to help make the meaning of a text clear eg capital letters, full stops
purpose	The reason for doing something
question	Asking for information or a response
recount	Writing about past events

reference	Place where a writer gained information
report	An informational text
research	The process of gathering information on a topic
resolution	The solving of a problem in a narrative
response	An author gives a personal opinion about something
review	Similar to a response, but the opinion is that of an expert
revision	Making changes to a piece of writing
rhetorical	Question where an answer is not expected
rhythm	The flow of words and phrases usually in poetry
scenarios	Possible situations
second person	Type of pronoun used when one character is speaking to another eg you
self reflection	An author thinking about their own writing
sentence	A group of words that conveys a complete thought or idea
sequence	The order of things
simile	Comparing things by saying one is like the other
slang	Casual language often used in speech eg I'm gonna catch ya.
slogan	A catchy phrase used in advertising
statement	A sentence that gives information
subject	The thing (noun) that a sentence is about
subjective	Written ideas that are based on opinion and not fact
subvert	To undermine or change someone else's ideas
summarise	To briefly note the main points
superlative	A way of comparing things by saying one is the best
technical	Things that are specific to a particular area such as mechanics or science
text	A piece of written or spoken communication
third person	Pronouns used when referring to a person other than the speaker or audience eg they
tone	The style of the writing
traditional	Long-held ideas and customs
verb	A word of action, speech or thought eg run, yell, believe
vocabulary	Words
voice	How the author uses their own personal style to influence the reader

INDEX